THE GROWING STRATEGIC THREAT OF ISIS

HEARING

BEFORE THE

COMMITTEE ON FOREIGN AFFAIRS
HOUSE OF REPRESENTATIVES

ONE HUNDRED FOURTEENTH CONGRESS

FIRST SESSION

FEBRUARY 12, 2015

Serial No. 114–17

Printed for the use of the Committee on Foreign Affairs

Available via the World Wide Web: http://www.foreignaffairs.house.gov/ or
http://www.gpo.gov/fdsys/

U.S. GOVERNMENT PUBLISHING OFFICE

93–284PDF   WASHINGTON : 2015

For sale by the Superintendent of Documents, U.S. Government Publishing Office
Internet: bookstore.gpo.gov   Phone: toll free (866) 512–1800; DC area (202) 512–1800
Fax: (202) 512–2104   Mail: Stop IDCC, Washington, DC 20402–0001

CONTENTS

THE GROWING STRATEGIC THREAT OF ISIS

THURSDAY, FEBRUARY 12, 2015

House of Representatives,
Committee on Foreign Affairs,
Washington, DC.

The committee met, pursuant to notice, at 10 o'clock a.m., in room 2172 Rayburn House Office Building, Hon. Ed Royce (chairman of the committee) presiding.

Chairman ROYCE. If members would take their seats. We are going to begin this hearing and I will ask all members to take their seats at this time.

This morning the committee continues our focus on the growing threat of ISIS. Of course, this hearing takes on added significance as yesterday the President requested that the Congress formally back military action against this jihadist organization, an organization which has beheaded Americans and which has sold and raped thousands of women in Syria.

And this is not a new threat for the members of this committee. One year ago, this committee took testimony from one of the few administration officials then sounding the ISIS alarm. That was Ambassador Brett McGurk.

He told us that that group's mission, that ISIS' mission was clear. As he said, they wanted to "carve out a zone of governing territory that would run from Baghdad to Syria to Lebanon." And, of course, at that point in time we were seeing a situation where ISIS was just beginning to expand into towns in Syria.

And members of this committee on both sides of the aisle called for air strikes against ISIS so that they could not begin that process of expansion.

Unfortunately, we went month after month after month. Town after town fell to ISIS across Syria and then across Iraq. Over the past 12 months, through a dozen hearings we have seen the ISIS threat only grow. Now we have three American hostages dead, including Kayla Mueller.

Not only have they been killed but ISIS has beheaded two Japanese hostages and immolated a downed Jordanian pilot for the world to see.

And this, again, is on top of what they have done in terms of raping, as I said, by now tens of thousands of women across Syria and other minorities, killing their husbands, raping the wives and the daughters.

This group occupies a vast territory. It holds an estimated $2 billion in assets. Now, I don't think there has ever been in history a terrorist organization as well funded as this terror group.

ISIS has used the ''virtual caliphate'' on the Internet to recruit foreign fighters at an ''unprecedented rate.'' Twenty thousand foreign fighters from 90 countries now make up the ranks of ISIS and, according to intelligence estimates, this includes 3,400 from the West and more than 150 Americans on the ground fighting for ISIS today.

Over the past year, this committee has pressed the administration to intensify and accelerate its response. Some pieces are being put together, but too slowly.

Of a 60-member coalition, 85 percent of all air strikes are from U.S. fighter jets, and this air campaign isn't pummelling the enemy as it should.

It is not intense enough. All of us were glad to see Iraq Prime Minister Maliki go, but with respect to reports of Shi'ite militias wreaking havoc, the jury is still out on the Abadi government's ability to field a competent and inclusive security force there.

The training and equipment of Iraqi forces also continues to lag, and we aren't likely see the 12 Iraqi brigades envisioned for several more months. Sunni tribal fighters are becoming more supportive of the national force, but the question is will they be in it for the long haul.

And after 6 months of fighting, the committee is still deeply concerned to receive reports that the Kurdish peshmerga are outgunned on the front lines, occasionally running out of ammunition on the front lines, underarmed and under equipped by the United States. This has to change.

Last fall, Congress voted to authorize training and equipping the Syrian opposition forces. But that is still not up and running and Assad looks more comfortable by the day. And, of course, this has left key allies in the region distraught and questioning the administration's strategy, as many here do.

Despite these problems, Kurdish forces on the ground and concentrated air support from coalition forces in the air helped take back Kobani. Some 6,000 fighters there were killed—ISIS fighters.

The Kurds have showed tremendous bravery and they deserve more and timely delivered aid to their cause of fighting ISIS.

Jordan's tragedy is galvanizing the coalition. Getting Jordan to step up its role in the air campaign and to commit ''thousands'' of troops to the border area with Iraq is a show of force.

Last week, the committee met with retired General John Allen, the State Department's lead to counter ISIS, and pledged our support to get Jordan the equipment that it needs in this fight. The UAE has also recommitted fighter planes to Jordan.

It is these Arab forces and voices that must be central in this fight. But they need to see and feel American leadership. I am pleased that the President has formally requested that Congress act on an authorization for use of military force against ISIS.

Now he needs to make the case to the American people and this committee as we work to examine this proposal in depth. This won't be easy.

But I am comforted by the fact that Ranking Member Engel and I are united in our desire to see bipartisan backing behind a proposal that ensures that the commander in chief has the authority needed to decisively defeat the enemy.

And so Mr. Engel is joining us a little later and I would like to now recognize the ranking member, Mr. Sherman of California, for his opening statement.

I thank our witnesses for being with us as well. Thank you.

Mr. SHERMAN. I think I am the second ranking member, Mr. Chairman. I view this as our first hearing on the President's request for an authorization to use military force.

I hope we focus on that request as the main duty of this committee and that we have not only hearings but that we move to a markup, and perhaps prior to moving to a markup we move to a discussion where members can take 5 minutes to explain what they would like to see in an ultimate resolution.

We are all aware of the evil of ISIS. ISIS almost asks us to take military action against them. If they had a Madison Avenue marketing firm and tried to say what can we do to provoke Americans, this is exactly what they would do.

What is interesting is that the Shi'ite alliance, what I would argue is at least as equal a danger, has done everything possible to avoid America taking military action. Whether they will bargain in good faith in Geneva I have no idea.

I haven't seen it yet. But they know that going to Geneva dampens down American concerns and, of course, they were quite successful in avoiding bombing of Syria by the United States and ultimately willing to give up most of their chemical weapons to do so.

Of course, America calls out for the immediate destruction of ISIS. I think we will see again in these hearings that to achieve that goal it would be extremely difficult, perhaps impossible and certainly involve tremendous American casualties.

We can contain ISIS. We can work for its eventual destruction. We can push things in the Middle East in the right direction, to some degree, without enormous American casualties.

But if we think we can remake the Middle East in our own image, we are certain to incur incredible American casualties and I am not sure that the Middle East will ever be what we want it to be.

Mr. Chairman, we had in this very room just yesterday hearings on Iran and I think that the Shi'ite alliance, led by Iran, and including many of the forces in Baghdad including the Shi'ite militias of Iraq, including Assad and Hezbollah, is more dangerous and more deadly than ISIS.

They have killed far more Americans, starting with the Beirut Marines back in the 1980s. They have carried on operations on virtually every continent. They are more capable of killing Americans in the homeland than is ISIS. They have killed far more people in the Middle East.

Assad alone has killed nearly 200,000, and if we are going to focus on ''destroying ISIS'' we shouldn't just focus on that. We need to ask what comes next—who fills the physical space, the ideological space and the cyber space.

Al-Qaeda is well positioned to fill the ideological space. They are an older organization but they may also learn social media to the level of ISIS. And as to the physical space, we see a Shi'ite alliance from Tehran to southern Lebanon that would be emboldened by the destruction of ISIS.

Believe it or not, I don't have a longer statement. I didn't—I expected Mr. Engel to be here. I will look down the road to see if someone wants me to yield them a minute. I see no one and I yield back to the chair.

Chairman ROYCE. Thank you, Mr. Chairman.

We go now to 1 minute for Ms. Ros-Lehtinen, chairman of the Subcommittee on the Middle East and North Africa.

Ms. ROS-LEHTINEN. Thank you so much, Mr. Chairman, and we all are deeply saddened by Kayla's appalling murder by ISIL terrorists. She made it her mission to care about humanity in a region that seems to no longer value human life and our prayers go out to her family.

The brutality of ISIL truly knows no bounds and this cancer continues to metastasize throughout the region. The President has finally given us a draft AUMF that may actually limit our engagement in the region.

So I look forward to a robust debate here in our committee on it. But I firmly believe that no matter what happens with the AUMF, solving the problem of ISIL cannot happen without simultaneously addressing the problems of Assad and Iran.

The administration's de facto partnership with Assad ensures that Syria will continue to be a terrorist breeding ground for groups like ISIL and we will never be victorious that way.

A big part of the administration's ISIL strategy is to train and equip a program that seems to enhance the capability of moderate Syrian opposition leaders. Yet, Mr. Chairman, that program hasn't really started yet.

The administration has said these fighters would be trained for defensive, not offensive, action and we are not engaging the Assad regime directly, only ISIL.

I worry that this policy is not going to be a victorious one. Thank you, Mr. Chairman.

Chairman ROYCE. Thank you. We go to Mr. Keating of Massachusetts, ranking member of the Terrorism Subcommittee, for his opening statement.

Mr. KEATING. Thank you, Mr. Chairman.

The confirmation of the death of American Kayla Mueller marks yet another tragic fatality at the hands of the terrorists, and while it is undoubtedly true that she would have gone on to personally enact great change, that her courage and empathy impacted far more lives than it can ever be counted and my prayers are with her loved ones at this time as I think all of us on the committee feel very strongly about.

Along with Kayla, our country has lost James Foley, Steven Sotloff, Peter Kassig, while our allies overseas have lost David Haines, Alan Henning, Haruna Yukawa, Kenji Goto, Moath al-Kasasbeh.

All of these people died tragically, and going forward it will be important for our continued response to contain a well-developed and multifaceted strategy with the support of our trusted partners within an international coalition.

As we now turn to the question of a new authorization for the use of military force, these are the metrics that I expect to be debated and continually reviewed and never forgotten.

It is critical and it is clear that we consider this matter as the most serious of decisions that all of us make as a congress.

Thank you, Mr. Chairman. With that, I yield back.

Chairman ROYCE. Thank you. We go now for 1 minute to Judge Ted Poe, chairman of the Subcommittee on Terrorism and Non-proliferation.

Mr. POE. Thank you, Mr. Chairman.

There is not a comprehensive strategy to defeat ISIS. The training and equipment of moderate rebels, whoever they may be, has not even started but when it does start it will not be enough to make a difference.

The rebels probably will end up fighting Assad, not ISIS. The air strikes on ISIS have taken a toll but no one believes they alone will be enough to defeat this group that is embedded in the local population.

The effort to turn Sunnis in Iraq against ISIS has also not shown any real significant progress. The Kurdish forces are the only group that has a record of battlefield successes against ISIS. They don't cut and run.

For some reason, we refuse to give them adequate weapons they need to fight against ISIS. We seem to be more concerned about Baghdad and even Turkey and what they think than about helping the Kurds.

My amendment to last year's intelligence authorization bill required a strategy to defeat ISIS. As we debate to give the President the power to go to war against ISIS, it would be nice if we knew exactly what the strategy was to win that war. What is the plan?

And I will yield back.

Chairman ROYCE. Thank you.

I will go to Mr. Deutch later when he joins the committee for his opening statement. But in the interim this morning we are pleased to be joined by a distinguished group of experts.

Ambassador James Jeffrey is a visiting fellow at the Washington Institute for Near East Policy and he previously served as Ambassador to Iraq and Turkey and to Albania.

Dr. Rick Brennan is the senior political scientist at the Rand Corporation and prior to joining Rand he served as a senior advisor to the U.S. military in Iraq for 5 years.

Dr. Dafna Rand is the Leon Panetta fellow and deputy director of studies at the Center for a New American Security. Previously, she served on the staff of the National Security Council. She was a professional staff member on the Senate Select Committee on Intelligence as well.

And we welcome them all and without objection the witnesses' full prepared statement will be made part of the record and the members here will have 5 legislative calendar days to submit statements and questions and any extraneous material for the record.

So, Ambassador Jeffrey, if we could start with you and ask you to summarize your remarks in 5 minutes. Thank you, sir.

STATEMENT OF THE HONORABLE JAMES F. JEFFREY, PHILIP SOLONDZ DISTINGUISHED VISITING FELLOW, THE WASHINGTON INSTITUTE FOR NEAR EAST POLICY

Ambassador JEFFREY. Thank you, Mr. Chairman, Mr. Sherman, members of the committee.

First of all, I think it is very important to note what we are doing today, as you said, considering an authorization for the use of military force.

It is fitting and just that the Congress as well as the executive branch undertakes such grave decisions as this and I am proud to be here today to provide whatever help I can.

Let me start with ISIS, and they have already gotten a lot of help from the three—four of you who have spoken. ISIS is a unique threat for all of the reasons you laid out, Mr. Sherman. I won't repeat them again.

But we haven't seen anything quite like this before, particularly the hold on territory, the people, the conventional military capabilities and its appeal to many people in the region.

But, secondly, ISIS is a threat in a unique sense because it is coming at a time of even more than usual disruption in the Middle East. It reflects the longer term trends and dangers in that region, a state system under extraordinary stress with its legitimacy questioned by the region's populations and with pan regional Islamic movements competing for the loyalty of these people.

It will require time and great effort by the governments and peoples of the region to free themselves of ISIS and of the thinking that is behind it, as Mr. Sherman discussed a few minutes ago.

In the end, they are going to have to do this. We can't. We can't tell them what their religion preaches and doesn't preach. We can't reach into the social structures of that part of the world. We have tried that. It didn't work very well.

But there is a point here and that is we can't expect them, much as they want to help us, to do all that much because they are engaged in conflicts and struggles, ideological and sometimes physical, within their own societies.

Thus, the President's goal to degrade and eventually destroy ISIS with America taking the lead is the correct mission. The campaign which the U.S. and a coalition of some 60 countries is implementing is basically sound.

The campaign has had considerable success of late from the pushback of ISIS in some areas to its containment in others and further success in the near future is actually quite possible.

Still, this campaign could well face tough sledding when the coalition begins major ground defensive operations and it hasn't done that yet. A lot of questions remain open.

As Representative Ros-Lehtinen said, we have got a lot of questions about Syria. What we have learned from Vietnam forward is you cannot defeat an insurgent group if it has a refuge in a neighboring country.

You have to do something about Syria and you can't do anything about Syria without having a better policy toward Assad.

We don't know whose boots on the ground are going to actually dig these guys out of places like Fallujah and Mosul. We don't know what the day after is going to look like. These are pretty tough questions.

In sum, we should not assume that time is on our side. Given this extraordinary threat, I urge the administration to move faster, take more risks and apply more resources. If our commanders on the ground want it, and that is the question, they should have the weapons systems they need.

If they need forward observers on the ground, if they need advisory teams out with local forces, they should get that despite the higher risks and costs.

Likewise, if our diplomats need more active top level U.S. pressure on various partners and players, including Iran, we should follow their advice.

In considering this authorization, I urge the Congress to give the administration maximum flexibility in timing and the use of forces. As one who has spent 4 years in Vietnam and Iraq, I am totally opposed to any enduring ground offensive presence if that means long-term counter insurgency campaigns.

We have tried them repeatedly. They haven't worked. But if necessary to meet the President's very valid mission of defeating ISIS, we should not rule out operations such as U.S. ground action to liberate Najaf and Fallujah in 2004.

While I hope it doesn't come to that, such a step could become necessary. The thing we should avoid above all else is putting limitations on our actions that will lead to us containing, not defeating and destroying, ISIS.

That will be seen by ISIS and many people in the region as a victory against the U.S., the West and the international order and it will stimulate support throughout the world for this awful organization.

Thank you very much, Mr. Chairman.

[The prepared statement of Ambassador Jeffrey follows:]

Assessing the Strategic Threat from ISIS

James F. Jeffrey
Philip Solondz Distinguished Visiting Fellow,
The Washington Institute for Near East Policy

Testimony submitted to the House Committee on Foreign Affairs
February 12, 2015

Mr. Chairman, Ranking Member Engel, it is a privilege to be here again before this committee, particularly to discuss a subject of such great importance to American interests and security as the strategic threat from the Islamic State of Iraq and al-Sham (ISIS).

The president's goal to degrade and eventually destroy ISIS is the correct mission. The campaign that the United States and a coalition of some sixty countries is implementing is basically sound, with direct military action, training and equipping local forces, building up political capacity with our partners in Iraq and Syria, cutting the flow of foreign fighters and funds to ISIS, combating the violent extremist ideology that fuels ISIS, and managing the human costs of the conflict. This campaign has had considerable success of late, from the pushback of ISIS in some areas, and its containment in others, to the redoubled commitment of our partners following the terrible ISIS execution of the Jordanian pilot.

Nevertheless, for reasons I will describe below, ISIS is a resilient and uniquely dangerous foe. Our campaign will be placed under stress when the coalition begins major ground-offensive operations. Military questions related to Syria, and political questions including "the day after" scenarios in both Syria and Iraq, are as yet unanswered, and the campaign runs some risk of settling into a containment mission that would eventually crater the coalition and lead to new ISIS threats. I therefore urge the administration to move faster, take more risks, apply more resources, and not assume "time is on our side." In the Middle East -- and world -- of today, it is not.

THE NATURE OF THE ISIS THREAT

ISIS is so dangerous because of its unique characteristics and its reflection of longer-term trends and dangers in the broader Middle East, from Pakistan to the Atlantic. Starting with the latter, we see a state system, as Henry Kissinger recently described, under extraordinary stress, with its legitimacy questioned by the region's populations. Their loyalty to any given state competes with both particularistic local and tribal ties, and pan-regional Islamic and, in the case of the Arab population, nationalistic impulses. ISIS, as the latest of a long series of pan-regional Islamic movements that espouse violence, like al-Qaeda and to some degree political Islamic movements such as the Islamic Republic of Iran and the Muslim Brotherhood, is embedded in various ways in the fabric of Middle Eastern society. It will require time and great effort by the governments and peoples of the region to free themselves of ISIS and its radical appeal, which can manifest itself in ever new ways, just as ISIS arose as a spinoff of the al-Qaeda movement.

But ISIS is not simply another manifestation of violent Islamic extremism. Its appeal to Muslims around the world, nihilist worship of violence, control over much territory and six or more million people, conventional as well as nonconventional military capabilities, and appeal as a caliphate all render it unique, and very difficult to combat. Its specific nature not only gives it significant resilience, but also an inevitable drive to inflict harm on the United States and other Western nations, either directly or by inspiring local jihadists.

Given its nature, the weaknesses of the Middle East state system which we are pushing to the forefront to deal with ISIS, and other threats to international security that the United States must simultaneously confront, I do not think a campaign of "strategic patience" is appropriate. ISIS may not have been successful in splitting the coalition with its horrific execution of the Jordanian officer, but it will continue its asymmetrical operations against the coalition, seek to expand its support among a small minority of Muslims, and exploit the Sunni-Shiite divide as the so-called champion of the Sunni side.

Under these circumstances, we should take more risks to accelerate offensive operations against ISIS. It is important, when these operations commence, that they succeed, to maintain the momentum of victory against ISIS begun at Mosul Dam and seen elsewhere, from Bayji refinery to Haditha Dam and Kobani. But we should accept more risk in terms of our own involvement to ensure our allies win on the ground in Mosul and elsewhere. The administration has, to its credit, done much since June to respond to and now contain ISIS. But it appears often to be applying the "strategic patience" doctrine to this conflict, limiting or closely monitoring military resources we are committing, and in particular treating the avoidance of any U.S. casualties as a strategic priority.

No one, including me, a former infantry officer, wants to see any American casualties. But while there are risks in a more robust policy, there are extraordinary risks in this campaign going forward at a simmer. Certain steps, if deemed wise by our military commanders, could make this campaign move forward faster and more effectively. It's their, not my, job to know which make sense in the specific situation, but the administration should not limit the use of those steps our commanders think useful. These could include a higher tempo of airstrikes, the deployment of Joint Terminal Attack Coordination teams, as well as advisory teams, down to the battalion level of units going on the offensive, using other weapons systems, such as U.S. army artillery and attack helicopter fires, given their role directly supporting ground operations, and providing heavier weapons to the Kurds.

THE POLITICAL CONTEXT

Just as the long-term response to the messages of ISIS and other Islamic extremist movements will depend primarily on political developments throughout the broader Middle East, so will the defeat of ISIS depend on political developments in Iraq and Syria.

In Iraq, the reconquest of Sunni Arab areas cannot be primarily the job of Kurdish Peshmerga units and certainly not Shiite militias. That effort has to combine local Sunni Arab levees, similar to the "awakening" movement of 2006-2008, and disciplined Iraqi regular army forces free of sectarian impulses, complemented by political outreach by Baghdad's largely Shiite Arab government to the Sunni Arabs and the Kurds. With much behind-the-scenes U.S. support, Iraqi prime minister Haider al-Abadi has made progress, sealing an oil deal with the Kurds, appointing and having confirmed a defense and interior minister, passing a budget for 2015 that incorporates the Kurdish oil deal, and gaining cabinet approval of new de-Baathification legislation and a national guard package, both requiring parliamentary approval but aimed at political reconciliation with Sunni Arabs. These efforts, while commendable, are not sufficient. Abadi faces threats from the Shiite political ranks, pressure from Iran, and the impact of dramatically falling oil revenues. Sunni Arab states must redouble the significant steps they have already taken to embrace this regime and work with their friends in the Iraqi Sunni community to win their support.

Over the longer term, reconciling all Iraq's religious and ethnic communities sufficiently to defeat, and keep Iraq permanently free of, ISIS and likely follow-on movements will require: first, decentralization including in the financial and security sectors, analogous to the conditions the Kurdistan Regional Government now enjoys, in Sunni and probably Shiite provinces; second, credible U.S. commitments of long-term engagement, including at least a limited number of American troops for training and airpower as we had planned in 2011; third, clarity with Iran that any effort by Tehran to dominate Iraq and drive the United States completely out will generate the next version of ISIS and eventually the breakup of the country, and a possible Shiite-Sunni conflagration. Iran cannot hold Iraq together, but it can drive it apart, and its policies of 2012-2014 almost did so.

In Syria, the administration's plans are just getting under way for a local defense force, seemingly to fight ISIS, not the Bashar al-Assad government. The administration is correct in prioritizing the "Iraq fight" over the Syria one, but the Syrian situation must eventually be dealt with if we are serious about defeating ISIS. Even a victory within Iraq will not last if ISIS retains a sanctuary next door, as we saw in the Korean and Vietnam wars, and in Iraq and Afghanistan. Furthermore, a serious alliance against ISIS built on Sunni Arab states and Turkey cannot hold together over the long term without a more forceful U.S. policy toward the Assad regime.

Chairman ROYCE. Thank you, Ambassador.
Doctor?

STATEMENT OF RICK BRENNAN, JR, PH.D., SENIOR POLITICAL SCIENTIST, RAND CORPORATION

Mr. BRENNAN. Chairman Royce, Ranking Member Engel and members of the committee, thank you for inviting me to speak to you about this important subject regarding the growing strategic threat of ISIS.

My argument today is straightforward and can be summarized in four key points. First, the key strategic threat that we face today is not from ISIS, al-Qaeda or any other group that is committing acts of violence or even genocide.

Rather, it is the radical Islamist ideology that gives these groups cause and for this we need a grand strategy that applies all means of U.S. national power to address it.

But to understand the scale of the challenge, one can look at the rapid expansion of the number of Sunni-inspired Salafi jihad groups during the last 25 years.

In 1988, only three groups existed. By 2010, the number of groups had expanded to 32. Then, as a result of the turbulence created by the Arab Spring, the number rapidly increased from 51— to 51 by 2013, a 62-percent increase in just 3 years.

It is also important to highlight that the Islamist movement has a Shi'a variant—the Islamic Republic of Iran. The theological interpretations of the Ayatollah Khomeini continues to inspire Iran's aggressive actions against the United States, Israel and the Sunni-led countries in the region.

Iran continues to be the largest state sponsor of terrorism in the world. Moreover, after the U.S. invasion of Iraq, Iran engaged in what could be called a covert war against the United States military and civilians operating in Iraq, using their proxy militias working at the behest of the Quds Force.

According to one military estimate, Iranian-supported militias likely caused as much as 50 percent of U.S. casualties in Iraq during the 8 years that we were there.

My second point is that ISIS is much more than a terrorist group. It is a revolutionary insurgency organization that seeks to establish new social, political and economic order without regard to internationally sanctioned state boundaries.

Its rapid success in Iraq and Syria has caused an explosion of volunteers from around the world who have joined the fight in places such as Syria, Iraq, Somalia, Libya, Afghanistan and Pakistan.

By 2012, with nearly 8 years of experience fighting both U.S. and Iraqi military forces and 2 years' experience fighting Syrian military and Iranian proxy militias, ISIS has become an experienced and hardened military force.

In January 2014, ISIS used the growing Sunni alienation within Iraq as an opportunity to seize control of Fallujah, located just 50 miles west of Baghdad. Following this early success, ISIS began an aggressive infiltration of Iraq that set the stage for the June offensive.

By August 2014, ISIS was in control of approximately 35,000 square miles of Iraq and Syria, a land mass that is approximately the size of the state of Indiana, and had begun to establish structures of governance and now calls itself the Islamic State.

My third point is that a number of factors contributed to the failure of the Iraqi military in 2014. Many of these were known in advance. One key factor was Prime Minister Maliki's efforts to consolidate and control the Iraqi military and security forces and replace incompetent officers with officers who were personally loyal to him.

A second factor was the endemic corruption that permeates the Iraqi political system and military establishment. Finally, it is also important to highlight that from 2009 to 2011 the U.S. military had consistently reported that the Iraq military had significant shortfalls in virtually all areas that were needed to conduct complex military operations without direct U.S. military assistance.

In part, this was the reason that General Lloyd Austin, General James Mattis and Admiral Michael Mullen recommended a residual force remain in Iraq of between 14,000 and 20,000.

My fourth point is that the administration's initial response to ISIS—the ISIS offensive in 2014 was a necessary first step to blunt the assault.

However, in my professional opinion as a career Army infantry officer and military planner who spent 5 years in Iraq between 2006 and 2011 as a senior advisor to the U.S. military, our current efforts are insufficient to enable Iraq to regain control of its territory and the key cities of Fallujah, Tikrit and Mosul and defeat ISIS either in Iraq or in Syria.

I believe that in addition to what the U.S. military is doing today the following would be required to achieve success.

First, develop a more robust advise and assist mission using conventional forces—the forces that we have there now are insufficient due to rapidly giving ISIS time to develop; second, enhance the size and scope of the command and control mission; third, employ U.S. special operations forces with attached tactical air control parties and other coalition ground forces down to the battalion level to enable them to assist in the conduct of an enhanced air campaign; and finally, to deploy U.S. special operations forces to conduct targeted counter terrorism missions in both Iraq and Syria.

In conclusion, there is an understandable reluctance to once again put American ground forces in Iraq. But if the threat to the region and the United States is as grave, using the wording of the AUMF, as the President indicated in the proposed AUMF, it is a mission that must be undertaken and, as Ambassador Jeffrey said, we should not have constraints on the AUMF and that we are going to have to be willing to use the ground forces if we are going to have success.

[The prepared statement of Mr. Brennan follows:]

The Growing Strategic Threat of Radical Islamist Ideology

Rick Brennan, Jr

RAND Office of External Affairs

CT-422

February 2015

Testimony presented before the House Foreign Affairs Committee on February 12, 2015

14

Published 2015 by the RAND Corporation
1776 Main Street, P.O. Box 2138, Santa Monica, CA 90407-2138
1200 South Hayes Street, Arlington, VA 22202-5050
4570 Fifth Avenue, Suite 600, Pittsburgh, PA 15213-2665
RAND URL: http://www.rand.org/
To order RAND documents or to obtain additional information, contact
Distribution Services: Telephone: (310) 451-7002;
Email: order@rand.org

Rick Brennan, Jr[1]
The RAND Corporation

The Growing Strategic Threat of Radical Islamist Ideology[2]

Before the Committee on Foreign Affairs
House of Representatives

February 12, 2015

Chairman Royce, Ranking Member Engel, and members of the Committee, thank you for inviting me to testify before you this morning regarding the growing strategic threat of ISIS.

My central argument today is that the threat posed by the Islamic State of Iraq and al-Sham (ISIS) and other radical Islamist organizations, both Sunni and Shi'a, continues to grow throughout the Middle East, North Africa, and other areas around the world. While the threat is often portrayed as terrorism, the true danger is the ideology that provides the logic of extremism, violence, and acts of inhumanity. While the direct threat to the United States homeland should not be overstated, some of these radical Islamist organizations pose an existential threat to countries in the Middle East, Near Asia, and North Africa. Today, ISIS controls a large swath of territory in both Syria and Iraq. The unprecedented success of ISIS is attracting large numbers of foreign fighters from Asia, North Africa, East Africa, Australia, Europe, Canada, and the United States. The Iraqi military is currently holding its own around Baghdad and southern Iraq. U.S. military actions in Iraq and Syria have helped to halt the advance of ISIS, especially assisting the Kurds in northern Iraq. Iranian-supported Shi'a extremist groups have provided critical support to the Iraqi government in stropping ISIS in Diyala, Ninewa, and Anbar provinces. Unfortunately, these Iranian-supported militias are also committing acts of violence against Sunni civilians, and pose a continuing threat to a sovereign Iraq that is free from undue Iranian influence.

I have divided my comments into four sections. The first provides an overview of the global threat posed by radical Islamist ideology from both the Sunni Salafist movement and the Iranian version of revolutionary Shi'ism. The second section explores the threat posed by ISIS in Iraq and Syria and throughout the Middle East, Africa, and both Pakistan and Afghanistan, where they are establishing networks and recruiting efforts. The third section will address the causes of the

---

[1] The opinions and conclusions expressed in this testimony are the author's alone and should not be interpreted as representing those of RAND or any of the sponsors of its research. This product is part of the RAND Corporation testimony series. RAND testimonies record testimony presented by RAND associates to federal, state, or local legislative committees; government-appointed commissions and panels; and private review and oversight bodies. The RAND Corporation is a nonprofit research organization providing objective analysis and effective solutions that address the challenges facing the public and private sectors around the world. RAND's publications do not necessarily reflect the opinions of its research clients and sponsors.

[2] This testimony is available for free download at http://www.rand.org/pubs/testimonies/CT422.html.

collapse of the Iraqi Army. Finally, the fourth section provides my assessment of how to best utilize the U.S. military in operations against ISIS.

The Global Threat Posed by Radical Islamist Ideologies

In February 1998, Osama bin Laden declared war on the United States and all other western liberal democracies in the statement entitled, "World Islamic Front Declaration of War against Jews and Crusaders." By issuing a fatwa calling for all Muslims to join the jihad against the West, bin Laden asserted both political and religious authority as the Sheikh of the World Islamic Front. The success of the 9/11 attacks increased his prestige in the Islamic world and encouraged other groups to affiliate with and swear allegiance to al-Qaeda. While bin Laden has been killed, the ideology of Salafi-jihadism continues to spread, and the global threat posed by al-Qaeda, ISIS, and affiliated groups is greater than ever.

Over the past decade, al-Qaeda has morphed into a highly decentralized organization while, simultaneously, the core ideology that provides the logic to Salafi-jihadism has both grown and become more decentralized and amorphous. The broader movement can be broken down into five basic categories. First is core al-Qaeda in Pakistan, led by Ayman al-Zawahiri, who continues to exert a leadership role in the movement. The second category includes groups that are formal affiliates who have sworn allegiance to al-Qaeda, such as al-Qaeda in the Arabian Peninsula (AQAP) operating in Yemen, al-Qaeda in the Islamic Maghreb (AQIM) operating in Algeria, and Jabhat al-Nusra (JN) operating in Syria. The third category is ISIS, an organization that shares a common ideology with al-Qaeda, but has claimed leadership of the Salafi-jihadist movement for itself and, therefore, is in direct competition with al-Qaeda and its affiliates. The fourth category is a large collection of groups that are committed to establishing an Islamic emirate, but have not sworn allegiance to either ISIS or al-Qaeda. The fifth category is composed of both networks and individuals who share the Salafi-jihadist ideology but are not directly connected to any particular group.[5]

To understand the scale of the challenge, one can look at the rapid expansion of the number of Salafi-jihadist groups over the past 25 years. In 1988, only three Salafi-jihadist groups were in existence. By 2001, the number of groups had expanded to 20. The growth in the number of groups continued at a steady rate until 2010. As a result of the turbulence created by the Arab Spring, the number jumped from 32 in 2010 to 51 in 2013.

---

[5] A previous RAND testimony conducted in March 2014 identified four tiers, but did not identify ISIS as a separate group. However, given the growth of ISIS during the intervening 11 months, it has emerged as a category in its own right. See Seth G. Jones, "The Extremist Threat to the U.S. Homeland: Addendum," Santa Monica, CA: RAND, 2014, p. 4.

This rapid rise in Salafi-jihadist groups corresponds to a comparable rise in the number of active Salafi-jihadist militants, with estimates indicating a range of between 9,000 and 22,000 in 2001 to between 30,000 and 88,000 in 2013.[6] The success of ISIS in 2014 continues to attract a growing number of fighters from around the world to join its efforts in such places as Syria, Iraq, Somalia, Libya, Afghanistan, and Pakistan.

While the tactic of terrorism is frequently the immediate threat focused upon by political leaders, I think it is critical to note that the ideology underlying these actions seeks revolutionary change of the existing political and social order. Thus, the strategic challenge of our generation isn't one particular group of insurgents or terrorists, it is the ideology that gives them cause. Defeating this ideology will require the development of a grand strategy that employs all elements of national power and influence.

It is also important to note that, while the focus of attention is on the Sunni Salafist movement, a Shi'a Islamist movement also exists with designs for dominance in the Middle East. In 1979, Ayatollah Ruhollah Khomeini established the Islamic Republic of Iran based on the principle of rule by Islamic jurists, or *velayat-e faqih*, where clerics serve as the head of state and Supreme Leader of Shi'a Islam. While there is no evidence that Iran seeks territorial gains, it is using its wealth and power to arm, train, and equip violent extremist groups throughout the region, enabling Iran to exert influence through both fear and intimidation. The theological interpretations of Ayatollah Khomeini provided the basis of the revolution that not only ousted the Shah of Iran but also inspired its aggressive stance against the United States, Israel, and most of the Sunni-led countries in the region. Iran continues to be one of the most active and prominent state sponsors of terrorism. Moreover, after the U.S. invasion of Iraq in 2003, Iran engaged in what could be viewed as a covert war against the United States in Iraq using its proxy militias. According to one U.S. military estimate, Iranian-supported militias likely caused as many as one-half of the U.S. casualties in Iraq.[7] As will be discussed below, it is the competition between the radical Shi'a Islamist movement led by Iran and the Sunni Salafi-jihadist organizations -- which received at least tacit support from Saudi Arabia, the Gulf States, and Turkey -- that has given rise to a regional crisis that amounts to a Sunni-Shi'a civil war.

---

[6] Seth G. Jones, *A Persistent Threat: The Evolution of al-Qa'ida and Other Salafi Jihadists*, Santa Monica, CA: RAND, 2014, p. 27.

[7] This staff estimate was developed by United States Forces-Iraq in 2011. See Brennan et.al, *Ending the U.S. War in Iraq: The Final Transition, Operational Maneuver, and Disestablishment of United States Forces-Iraq*, Santa Monica, CA: RAND, 2014, p. 125.

The Threat Posed by ISIS in Iraq, Syria, and throughout the Middle East

From March to July 2011, the revolutionary wave of protests and demonstrations known as the Arab Spring began to challenge the regime of Bashar al-Assad in Syria. Despite early attempts to pacify the majority Sunni populace, the Syrian government soon resorted to police and military brutality. As the protests grew, Iran and Russia began to provide military assistance to maintain the stability of the Assad regime. Upon the departure of U.S. forces from Iraq in 2011, Iran became more active in defending the Syrian regime and began sending a large amount of arms, munitions, and supplies to support the Syrian military. In early 2012, Iran also deployed a large number of Quds Force personnel to coordinate, direct, and support a ground force campaign using its proxy militias -- Lebanese Hezbollah and a number of Iraqi militias, including Kata'ib Hezbollah, Asa'ib al-Haq, and others. Together, Iran and its proxies targeted the al-Qaeda affiliated al-Nusra Front and the remnants of al-Qaeda in Iraq (AQI), then calling itself the Islamic State of Iraq (ISI).

While the Assad regime had allowed AQI/ISI to use Syria as a safe-haven to arm, train, equip, and support groups that conducted terrorist operations within Iraq between 2004 and 2011, ISI quickly became the most powerful extremist militia challenging the Assad regime. With nearly eight years of experience fighting U.S. and Iraqi forces, ISI had evolved into a hardened military force that that not only challenged the Syrian military, but also was able to hold its own against Iranian proxy militias.[8] In addition to confronting the Assad regime, ISI started to increase the number of operations it was conducting within Iraq. In what ISI called the "Breaking of the Walls Campaign," the number of attacks within Iraq increased from 75 per month in 2011 to 140 per month by the fall of 2012.[9]

At the same time that ISI was increasing its attacks, Iraqi Prime Minister Nouri al-Maliki began taking actions that alienated large segments of the Sunni populace, creating a breeding ground for a new Sunni insurgency in Anbar, Salah ad Din, and Ninewa provinces. By January 2014, ISI had used the growing Sunni disenfranchisement as an opportunity to seize control of Fallujah, a city located less than 50 miles west of Baghdad. Following this success, ISI began an aggressive infiltration into Iraq that set the stage for the June offensive that seized Mosul and most of the Tigris River Valley from Mosul to Samarra, located 78 miles north of Baghdad. Simultaneously, ISI launched a major offensive in the north that pushed to the outskirts of Erbil in the Kurdish region. By August 2014, ISI was in control of approximately 35,000 square miles of Iraq and Syria

---

[8] Iran's role in the Syrian conflict is documented in Brennan et al., *Ending the U.S. War in Iraq*, pp. 301–304.

[9] Brennan et al., *Ending the U.S. War in Iraq*, p. 304.

-- a landmass approximately the size of the state of Indiana -- and had begun to establish structures of governance, calling itself the Islamic State of Iraq and the Levant.

The Causes of the Rapid Collapse of the Iraqi Army

During the eight years that the U.S. military was in Iraq, a primary goal was to develop a professional and competent Iraqi military. Billions of U.S. taxpayer dollars were spent to ensure that the Iraqi military could operate without U.S. assistance. Yet, in June of 2014, we witnessed the near total collapse of four of Iraq's 12 army divisions when confronted by the ISIS assault.

There are several factors that led to the collapse of the Iraqi military, many of which were caused or aggravated by actions taken by Prime Minister Maliki to solidify power and create a "praetorian guard" to guarantee his continued rule. For example, starting in 2007, Maliki centralized his control of the Iraqi intelligence and security forces, replacing competent officers with officers personally loyal to him. After the 2010 election, Maliki refused to appoint permanent ministers of Defense, Interior, and Intelligence, electing to control each of these ministries himself through an extra-constitutional organization called the Office of the Commander-in-Chief. This resulted in an overly centralized command structure where leaders at all levels were reluctant to act without instructions.

A second factor that led to the collapse of the Iraqi army was endemic corruption that permeates the political system and military establishment. For example, a common practice was for military commanders to overly report the number of soldiers present for duty so they could pocket the extra pay. While this practice was widely known to occur, the government did little to stop the thievery, resulting in a large number of Iraqi units being undermanned at the time of the ISIS assault.

Finally, it is important to highlight that from 2009 through 2011 the U.S. military in Iraq consistently reported that the Iraqi military had significant shortfalls that would hinder its capability to conduct operations against external threats. These assessments stated that the Iraqi security forces suffered from weak intelligence collection, analysis, and sharing; an inability to sustain combat operations; poor maintenance of equipment and weapons; the lack of a well-developed training program; poor command and control of its forces; a lack of sufficient intelligence, surveillance, and reconnaissance (ISR) assets; and a very limited ability to conduct counterterrorism operations without direct U.S. support. The Iraqi air force was even worse off: It could not do much besides transport forces from one air base to another, and it had no ability to provide lethal support to Iraqi ground forces in combat.[10] It was because of these shortfalls that General Lloyd Austin, General James Mattis, and Admiral Michael Mullen recommended a residual force of between 14,000 and 20,000 be retained in Iraq beyond 2011.[11]

The Role of the U.S. Military in the War Against ISIS

As ISIS moved toward the city of Erbil in July 2014, President Obama decided to employ U.S. airpower to support the Iraqis. In addition, the President authorized the deployment of a limited number of military personnel to help train four Iraqi brigades, enhance security of the U.S. embassy and facilities, provide intelligence to Iraqi forces, and help the Iraqis plan operations to degrade and ultimately defeat ISIS. The President also placed a cap of no more than 1,500 troops to be deployed in non-combat roles.

The actions by the administration in Iraq are a necessary first step, but, in my professional opinion as a former military planner, will likely be insufficient to ensure Iraq has the capabilities to defeat ISIS. Given what is known about the Iraqi security forces -- and based solely upon my experience in the U.S. military and not based on any RAND analysis -- I believe that in addition to what the U.S. military is doing today, the following will be required to achieve success:

1. Develop a more robust advise and assist mission using conventional forces. The size of the force package deployed today is not large enough to do the mission rapidly, and this is giving time for ISIS to grow and consolidate its gains in Iraq and Syria.
2. Enhance the size and scope of the command and control mission inside Iraq to help the Iraqis coordinate the efforts of the broader coalition, a capability the Iraqi military does not currently have.
3. Employ U.S. special operations forces, with attached Tactical Air Control Parties (TACPs) and Forward Air Controllers (FACs), to accompany Iraqi, Peshmerga, and other coalition ground forces as necessary to help facilitate the effective employment of an enhanced U.S.-led air campaign.
4. Deploy U.S. counterterrorism forces to work with Iraqi special operations forces and special forces from other countries in the region to conduct targeted counterterrorism operations in both Iraq and Syria.

---

[10] For a more thorough discussion of the shortfalls in the Iraqi security sector, see Brennan et al., *Ending the U.S. War in Iraq*, pp. 157–202. See also Rick Brennan, "Withdrawal Symptoms: The Bungling of the Iraq Exit," *Foreign Affairs*, November/December 2014, pp. 25–36.

[11] Brennan, "Withdrawal Symptoms," pp. 33.

There is an understandable reluctance to once again put additional U.S. ground forces in Iraq but, at the same time, it is worth noting that this hesitation is likely to be interpreted by regional partners as a lack of commitment, making the challenge of building a regional solution that includes the employment of coalition ground forces all the more difficult. This is not to say that the United States should use conventional forces in a combat role. However, those U.S. special operations personnel serving as advisors to front-line coalition forces could find themselves in a combat situation.

The number of service members required to effectively conduct and support these missions (advise and assist, command and control coordination assistance, forward air control, and counterterrorism) would be relatively small. Based on work I did for the U.S. military while deployed to Iraq as a senior civilian advisor, I believe the requirement would likely be in the range of 5,000-8,000 troops. This estimate could vary depending on changes in the situation or mission, but would not be the type of large-scale operation that existed in Iraq prior to 2012. While small in number, the presence of U.S. forces would serve as combat multipliers; magnifying the capabilities of the Iraqi military, Peshmerga, and potential ground forces supplied by neighboring countries -- such as Jordan. Again, based on my former military experience and not on any RAND analysis, I believe that this type of enhanced U.S. military participation and partnership is something that will be required if Iraq is to successfully regain control of lost territory, especially the cities of Fallujah, Tikrit, and Mosul.

Concluding Thoughts

Since the 1970s, both Democratic and Republican administrations have accepted the responsibility for helping to ensure continued regional security in the Middle East. Close military-to-military relationships have been developed with the majority of countries in the region, including Saudi Arabia, Jordan, Egypt, and all of the Gulf states, using forward military presence, efforts to build partner capacity, and other forms of political, economic, and military cooperation. The threat posed by ISIS provides an opportunity to employ a regional coalition using the partnerships that have been nurtured over the past 40 years. Unfortunately, the withdrawal of U.S. forces from Iraq in 2011 not only created a power vacuum that has been exploited by ISIS and Iran, but it may also have contributed to the perception by many of our regional partners that the United States is disengaging from the Middle East. Again, my recommendations today are not based on work that I have done at RAND. But, based on my experience as a former military officer who spent five years deployed in Iraq as a senior civilian advisor to the U.S. military, I believe that the employment of U.S. military forces for the types of missions I have identified would go a long way toward demonstrating U.S. resolve and commitment in a manner that would facilitate building the type of coalition necessary to defeat ISIS.

Chairman ROYCE. Thank you, Dr. Brennan.

STATEMENT OF DAFNA H. RAND, PH.D., LEON E. PANETTA FELLOW AND DEPUTY DIRECTOR OF STUDIES, CENTER FOR A NEW AMERICAN SECURITY

Ms. RAND. Thank you. Chairman Royce, Ranking Member Engel, members of the esteemed committee, thank you for holding this hearing and for inviting me to testify on the timely topic.

I would like to discuss three key questions that Americans are asking today about the AUMF and the threat that ISIS poses. The questions are pretty simple. They come down to what, why and how.

What is ISIS, they are asking. Although ISIS has its roots—al-Qaeda offshoot—in both its brutality and its battlefield successes, it represents a new type of threat. I will just mention three particular characteristics of ISIS because many have been articulated already by the members of this committee.

First, the savagery is at the core of the ideology. While al-Qaeda justifies individual suicide bombing attacks against civilians through fatwas explaining the conditional necessity, ISIS has adopted an entirely new ideology, manipulating select stories from Islamic history and modern jihadi texts to redefine jihad.

It has generated a blanket justification for violence including against women and children. Second, the group, as already mentioned, has adopted a military doctrine that is not based on the typical terrorist logic of the weak fighting the powerful.

Instead, ISIS aspires to fight states and their militaries as a peer. It believes in the necessity of full blown military campaigns and seeks to control as much territory as possible.

And finally, ISIS is not bound by the same political concerns or need to appeal to the public. We just saw that with the horrific images of the Jordanian pilot who was immolated by ISIS last week.

With a violent approach that has little regard for political strategy, ISIS is now a decentralized defused aspirational social movement that follows few orders and few chains of command.

The second question that Americans are asking is why does this matter to us, to our interests, to our role in the world. After 14 years of deep U.S. military engagement in the broader military East, Americans have a right to a strong, clear and convincing answer to this question—why should our resources and our U.S. military be deployed in this fight.

The best answer is that we are trying to degrade and destroy ISIS to achieve three very specific national security objectives—to prevent ISIS attacks against the United States and our direct interests abroad, to degrade the organization's ability to control populated areas from which it can recruit foreign fighters and to protect the sovereignty of U.S. partners against ISIS.

The third question is the most complicated and we will discuss it today. The question is how—how do we defeat ISIS or at least how do we degrade this threat enough to achieve the three basic goals that I just enumerated.

The overall strategy to defeat and degrade ISIS will necessarily entail coercive and noncoercive tools of U.S. statecraft. In other words, the use of U.S. military power is just one tool and it must be integrated with a set of other tools, particularly multilateral and bilateral diplomacy.

For example, perhaps the greatest success we have seen so far against ISIS is this administration's ability to mobilize a diverse and significant international coalition. Over 60 nations have not just committed to fighting the threat in words but they are acting.

They are participating in the air strikes, they are countering ISIS' financing, they are stopping the flow of foreign fighters and they are responding to the humanitarian catastrophe.

The use of military force is therefore a necessary but not sufficient part of the strategy. The draft language offered by the President yesterday, in my view, suggests a very carefully tailored strategy based directly on the advice and counsel of the military leaders and also the evidence of what is working so far in the past 5 months.

What have we seen in the past 5 months that is effectively degrading ISIS' capabilities in Iraq and Syria? We have seen evidence that since September we are making significant progress in degrading ISIS by using a combination of air strikes by the coalition coordinated with local forces on the ground.

Through this partnership approach, we have eliminated nearly 6,000 ISIS fighters in Iraq and 1,000 in Syria. We are diminishing supply lines and manpower and, probably most importantly, we have decreased the group's momentum.

We have three main military partners on the ground. We have the Iraqi security forces, the Kurdish fighters, as has been mentioned associated with the KRG, and then we have our Syrian opposition forces which include both Arab and Kurdish factions.

These groups are committed to fighting ISIS and have deep connections with the local populations in the region. They are best placed to understand the social-political contacts that has allowed ISIS to incubate itself and thrive in these tribal areas in the first place.

Therefore, in conclusion, I believe that a limited tailored use of U.S. military force in this operation reflects a larger strategy, one that has preliminarily been working, a strategy that prioritizes the role of the partners on the ground in ultimately defeating ISIS and filling in the vacuums left behind upon ISIS' retreat.

The limited tailored approach suggests to the war-weary American public and the Muslim world that we are not interested in another decade-long U.S. presence on the ground in the heart of the Middle East. Degrading ISIS and reducing the threat it poses simply does not require that kind of approach.

In conclusion, force is one element of our strategy and we should use it wisely, judiciously and in a way that is most effective. This one element is certainly insufficient to degrade ISIS in a sustainable long-term manner.

So I urge you, even as Congress is focused on the appropriate use of force, it must not lose sight of the larger political strategy and the urgent diplomatic work that will be necessary.

I look forward to your questions so that we can talk more about these nonmilitary objectives which differ across three distinct theaters—Iraq, Syria and in the broader global context to diminish the appeal of ISIS ideology.

Thank you.
[The prepared statement of Ms. Rand follows:]

"The Growing Strategic Threat of ISIS"

Testimony Before the House Committee on Foreign Affairs

Dr. Dafna H. Rand
Deputy Director of Studies and Leon E. Panetta Fellow, Center for a New American Security

February 12, 2015

Mr. Chairman, Mr. Ranking Member, Members of the Committee, thank you for holding this hearing. The American people remain concerned about the threat posed by the Islamic State of Iraq and the Levant (ISIL), and their government's response. Today I'd like to touch briefly on the nature of the threat and then focus specifically on the diplomatic aspects of the strategy to combat it. How we deploy our non-military tools will be just as important as the use of force to degrade and to defeat ISIL, an organization that is part army, part vicious ideology, and part exploitative social movement.

Use of Force Against ISIL: An Evolved Threat

A number of distinct characteristics of ISIL require the use of military force in a way that is tailored to the threat posed by the group to American interests. First, ISIL's savage tactics are at the very core of its ideology. While al-Qaeda justifies individual suicide bombing attacks against civilians and civilian areas through fatwas explaining the conditional necessity, ISIL has adopted a new ideology, manipulating select stories from Islamic history and modern jihadi texts to redefine jihad and to generate a blanket justification for violence, including against women and children.[1] Second, the group has adopted a military doctrine that is not based on the typical terrorist logic of the weak fighting the powerful. ISIL aspires to fight states and their militaries as a peer. To defeat states, ISIL calculates that random acts of violence are insufficient. It believes in the necessity of full-blown military campaigns.[2] Finally, ISIL believes in the importance of escalatory, sensationalist acts of violence intended to shock and deter the public. The Jordanian people, and the world, were horrified by the images of the Jordanian pilot immolated by ISIL. Yet the group considers such public savagery core to its approach, rather than a risky act that is likely to alienate potential supporters in the Muslim world.[3]

In addition, ISIL leaders refuse to follow traditional chains of command. In early 2013, the group defied orders from al-Qaeda's leader, Ayman al-Zawahiri, to kill fewer civilians in Syria. These tensions led to an al-Qaeda communiqué issued in February 2014 disavowing any connection

---

[1] Hassan Hassan, "ISIS has reached new depths of depravity. But there is a logic behind it," *The Guardian*, February 8, 2015, http://www.theguardian.com/world/2015/feb/08/isis-islamic-state-ideology-sharia-syria-iraq-jordan-pilot.
[2] Terrence McCoy, "The Battle for Kobane and the Islamic State's 'Swarm' War Strategy," *The Washington Post*, October 8, 2014. http://www.washingtonpost.com/news/morning-mix/wp/2014/10/08/the-battle-for-kobane-and-the-islamic-states-swarm-war-strategy/.
[3] Michael W.S. Ryan, "From Theory to Action: The Rationale Behind the Re-Establishment of the Caliphate," Jamestown Foundation Terrorism Monitor, 12 no 15, July 25, 2014,
http://www.jamestown.org/programs/tm/single/?tx_ttnews%5Btt_news%5D=42670&cHash=d35aeb2c012e5fc38e5a06df2e2a4cc8#.VNtWVy6xWfg.

with ISIL because of the latter's excessive violence, including brutality towards its competitors within the armed Syrian opposition.[4]

These characteristics of ISIL suggest the need for a new strategy to defeat it. It is unlikely we will ever destroy the organization entirely. However, limited U.S. military force is a necessary, though certainly not sufficient, element of the larger strategy to limit ISIL's operational capacity. The use of American military force should be used: a) to prevent ISIL attacks against the United States; b) to protect the sovereignty of U.S. partners against ISIL; and c) and to degrade this organization's ability to control populated areas, from which it can recruit foreign fighters and generate global momentum.

The most important limitation on the use of military force against ISIL is a sunset clause that would require the renewal of authorization in a few years. This is a first order requirement because, to keep our strategy focused, over the next few years we will need to re-evaluate the geographical boundaries of the enemy's operations, the definition of the enemy, the duration of the fight, and the particular military operations that are successfully countering the threat. Because of the importance of oversight and the likelihood that facts on the ground will change, any authorization should include robust reporting requirements that ask for clear metrics of success, U.S. and allied progress in the military campaign against ISIL, and progress in our efforts to build the capacity of our partners. These reporting requirements should include information on civilian casualties and any indication of popular blowback and increasing anti-Americanism in the Arab and Muslim worlds as a direct result of our military efforts.

It is important that we explicitly commit to the limitation on the use of extended ground forces in the operation. First, limiting the use of U.S. force underscores how our strategy prioritizes the role of the partners on the ground in ultimately defeating ISIL and filling in the vacuums left upon ISIL's retreat. Second, this limitation makes it clear to the war-weary American public and the Muslim world that we are not interested in another decade-long U.S. presence on the ground in the heart of the Middle East. Degrading ISIL and reducing the threat it poses simply do not require such an approach.

In Syria and Iraq, we may need to target groups associated but not self-identified as ISIL, but we must be careful not to broaden the aperture too widely, casting too wide a net in targeting all associated groups of ISIL operating globally. Our ability to degrade ISIL in Syria, Iraq, and elsewhere and our capacity to mobilize the international community against this threat will be stronger if we limit the authorized global target to ISIL only.

The Centrality of Diplomacy

As it should, this Congress will now focus on the proper use of American military force to counter ISIL. Nonetheless, kinetic operations are only one component of a larger political approach. Our success depends as much on mobilizing our partners to fight ISIL – and helping them to sustain their own efforts over time – as it does on immediate military strikes. First, we

---

[4] Liz Sly, "Al-Qaeda disavows any ties with radical Islamist ISIS group in Syria, Iraq," *Washington Post*, February 3, 2014, http://www.washingtonpost.com/world/middle_east/al-qaeda-disavows-any-ties-with-radical-islamist-isis-group-in-syria-iraq/2014/02/03/2c9afc3a-8cef-11e3-98ab-fe5228217bd1_story.html.

need military partners on the ground in Iraq and Syria so that there are viable governing entities that can control territory in those areas where ISIL's grip has been weakened. Politically, we need partners in the Arab world who are willing to expend energy and political capital to counter ISIL's ideology. And, internationally, we need to leverage our role in regional and multilateral institutions to forge cooperation among states on issues such as border security and terrorism financing. It is important for Congress to support the role of diplomacy at the heart of the counter-ISIL strategy.

Indeed, the Administration's most significant success thus far has been in the realm of multilateral diplomacy: the U.S.-led Coalition of over 60 countries has enhanced regional and global U.S. leadership and advanced our concrete objectives in degrading ISIL. We have a diverse roster of Coalition partners and the Arab states' military contributions to the campaign is significant.[5] Four Arab nations are participating in airstrikes in Syria with us, for instance.[6] The degree of global cooperation forged by this Coalition on issues such as border security and terrorism finance is without parallel since September 11, 2001.

In Iraq, Syria, and in the global context, we should employ different diplomatic tools and levers, tied together through the consistency of U.S. leadership. We must degrade and ultimately destroy ISIL in all three places, but the ways to achieve this objective now differ among each of these theaters.

Degrading ISIL in Iraq

The way forward to stop ISIL's advance in Iraq is the most straightforward. There is evidence that the Coalition air campaign, combined with cooperation with local forces on the ground, has significantly slowed ISIL's ability to seize new territory, allowing the Kurdish regions of Iraq to rebuild their defenses, including near Erbil, and giving the new Iraqi government and its security forces an opportunity to train and prepare for longer term counter-terrorism operations. ISIL in western Iraq is not going away in the short- to medium-term, but the grave threat ISIL posed to all of Iraq in 2014 has subsided. In Iraq, approximately 6,000 ISIL fighters have been killed,

---

[5] For example, the Jordanian Air Force, which launched a number of sorties and helped to destroy ISIL logistics centers, has increased its military efforts in the aftermath of a Jordanian pilot being captured and burned alive. Saudi Arabia has launched airstrikes in Syria and it has provided $500 million to the UN and humanitarian aid agencies. The United Arab Emirates has been referred to as the "Sparta on the Gulf" for its military role in airstrikes against ISIS.. Bahrain has sent F16s to launch airstrikes in Syria as well.
See: William Booth and Taylor Luck, "Jordan Says its Airstrikes are Targeting Islamic State Leadership," *The Washington Post*, February 8, 2015, http://www.washingtonpost.com/world/middle_east/jordan-says-its-airstrikes-are-targeting-islamic-state-leadership/2015/02/08/431cfc88-63f0-4acd-b005-94d6661aac3a_story.html; Mohammed Daraghmeh, "Jordanians Say 56 Airstrikes Against ISIS are the Beginning," *Business Insider*, February 8, 2015, http://www.businessinsider.com/jordan-says-56-airstrikes-against-isis-are-the-beginning-2015-2; Mohsin Ali and Yarno Ritzen, "Interactive: Countries Countering ISIL," *Al-Jazeera*, December 16, 2015, http://www.aljazeera.com/indepth/interactive/2014/10/isil-us-syria-airstrike-coalition-uac-saudi-2014101142731382476.html;; Ian Black, "UAE's Leading Role Against ISIS Reveals its Wider Ambitions," *The Guardian*, October 30, 2015, http://www.theguardian.com/world/2014/oct/30/uae-united-arab-emirates-leading-player-opposition-isis-middle-east; Ashley Fantz, "Who's Doing What in the Coalition Battle Against ISIS," *CNN*, October 7, 2014, http://www.cnn.com/2014/10/06/world/meast/isis-coalition-nations/.
[6] Gen. John Allen, "A Global, Coordinated, and Enduring Response," (Washington Institute for Near East Policy, Washington, February 2, 2015),
https://www.washingtoninstitute.org/uploads/Documents/other/AllenStatement20150202.pdf.

including half of the group's known leadership. The airstrikes have diminished ISIL's command and control structure and its supply and logistical lines.[7] ISIL today in Iraq is facing a manpower drain and a limitation in its ability to move fighters around the battlefield.[8]

Absent political progress these gains are reversible, however.

Even as General Allen and others continue to oversee Coalition efforts to combat ISIL in Iraq, the strategic focus should shift to the internal politics of the country. The Coalition is making progress retraining the Iraqi Security Forces (ISF) to fight ISIL, and many member nations are contributing trainers and hardware assistance. The central objective in this effort, however, should be a focus on retraining the ISF so that it eventually becomes a multiethnic, inclusive, professional force, which can protect all Iraqis, regardless of sect or regional origin. To do so, we need to consider how the ISF fractured in the first place, how it was susceptible to politicization, and why it remains so vulnerable to Iranian influence. The ISF's will and capabilities, and its integration with police and other security services across the country, will determine the endurance of the military gains against ISIL that the Coalition and its Iraqi partners are achieving.

Outreach to Sunni Iraqi leaders should be a second critical priority for U.S. and allied diplomatic efforts. It will be difficult to replicate the successes of the Sunni Awakening, but we nonetheless must encourage, support, and engage a new generation of "Sons of Iraq."[9] To do so, the United States must help the Iraqi government, as well as other Arab allies, to bring into the fold those Sunni leaders with credibility among their tribes who may have the local clout to disavow ISIL and other bad actors.

Implementing structural and institutional guarantees for Sunni communities will be a fundamental component of the political effort to build trust in the Sunni heartland. Key guarantees should involve at least three issues: ensuring that Sunni communities receive profits from national oil revenues; institutionalizing and codifying government programs and subsidies expected by the Sunni communities; and improving communal policing. Guarantees from Baghdad and from the international community can help to reassure the Sunni community that the human rights abuses of the Maliki era, which overwhelmingly victimized Sunnis, do not repeat themselves under the current al-Abadi and future governments in Baghdad.

Finally, U.S. diplomacy and leadership will be necessary to help the Iraqi economy rebound, particularly because the depressed global oil price is hurting the central Iraqi government's

---

[7] Ibid. The commander of the Royal Jordanian Air Force, Gen. Mansour Al-Jbour, estimates that 20 percent of ISIL's military capabilities have been destroyed and approximately 7,000 ISIL fighters have been killed since Coalition airstrikes began in September 2014. See: "Jordan: ISIS Lost 20% of Its Military Capabilities," Al-Arabiya, February 8, 2015, http://english.alarabiya.net/en/News/middle-east/2015/02/08/Jordan-ISIS-lost-20-of-its-military-capabilities.html.

[8] Suleiman Al-Khalidi, "Islamic State Pulls Forces and Hardware from Syria's Aleppo: Rebels," Reuters, February 9, 2015; Harvey Morris, "

[9] The Sons of Iraq were Iraqi Sunni tribal militias, located in western Iraq's Anbar governorate, that were part of a local response against the excesses of ISIL's predecessor, the al-Qaeda affiliate the Islamic State of Iraq (ISI). U.S. military forces cooperated with the "Sons of Iraq" (SOI) to drastically reduce ISI's power in western Iraq. See: Myriam Benraad, "Iraq's Tribal 'Sahwa': Its Rise and Fall." Middle East Policy Council, 18 no.1 (November 2011).

revenue. The United States should leverage the Coalition as a source of reconstruction and assistance funds for the more than 2,047,000 refugees and internally displaced persons in Iraq, including the approximately 300,000 Syrian refugees, and to help the Iraqi government pay for its security and other needs.[10] Here, Iraq's Gulf neighbors should consider the recuperation of the Iraqi economy as a direct interest and investment.

Reducing ISIL's Power in Syria

On one hand, the United States and its allies have, since last fall, degraded ISIL's strength in Syria. By providing airstrike cover to Kurdish and Arab fighters at Kobani, they thwarted a massive ISIL assault there and killed nearly 1,000 ISIL fighters. North of Aleppo, Coalition efforts against ISIL have allowed the Syrian opposition to hold their ground and have forced ISIL to stage tactical withdrawals from some of the territory it controls in the Aleppo governorate.[11]

On the other hand, efforts to reduce more definitively ISIL's influence and extricate it from the Syrian territory it now rules will ultimately depend on the chances of de-escalating the four year-old conflict between the opposition and the Syrian regime of Bashar al-Assad.[12] ISIL and its ideological peers will never be defeated in Syria until there is a diminution in the civil conflict that has persisted since 2011. The best case scenario is a reduction in the fighting based on the promise of a political horizon that shepherds a fair transition process toward a post-Assad future. A transition process will require the opposition and the Assad regime to compromise on transitional justice mechanisms and on a plan to recognize the local governance systems in place across Syria, where the regime now holds no more than 30 percent of the territory containing 40 percent of the population. Any agreement must be based on a power-sharing system in Damascus that may have to include parts of the Assad regime, including Alawis, with opposition representatives, as well as decentralization mechanisms in the North and the South of Syria.

Therefore, reducing ISIL's power in Syria will require international diplomacy in the near term, including working toward a Geneva III international negotiation. Such negotiations could commence if there are signs that Tehran and Moscow recognize the danger of the status quo. Both of these key patrons of Syria must realize that the stalemate between the moderate oppositionists and the regime is advantaging ISIL – to the detriment of their own security interests.

---

[10] Antonio Ponce, "Refugees in Iraqi Camps Face Harrowing Winter," Huffington Post, January 24, 2015; "UNHCR 2015 Country Operations Profile: Iraq," United Nations High Commissioner for Refugees, January 2015, http://www.unhcr.org/pages/49e486426.html.

[11] Suleiman Al-Khalidi, "Islamic State Pulls Forces and Hardware from Syria's Aleppo: Rebels," Reuters, February 9, 2015.

[12] In Syria, the United States will need to establish a procedure for identifying the potential threat to the U.S. homeland from ISIL's competitors in the militant Salafist movement, such as the al-Qaeda affiliate Jabhat al-Nusra. For this reason, the authorization for military force should be broader than ISIL alone in Syria. U.S. military planners and civilians will have to carefully navigate between lumping together all dangerous terrorist groups affiliated with ISIL as appropriate targets in Iraq and Syria and clearly identifying those posing a direct and immediate threat to the United States and its partners. See Tom Coghlan and Hannah Lucinda Smith, "Al-Qa'ida Branch in Syria Carves Out Mini-State of its Own," The Australian, February 7, 2015; Liz Sly, "U.S.-Backed Syrian Rebels Routed by Fighters Linked to Al-Qaeda," The Washington Post, November 2, 2014.

Second, defeating ISIL is a top priority for U.S. interests, but the United States must continue to prosecute its efforts against the group in a way that bolsters the more moderate opposition to Assad, as opposed to the regime. We must counter any regime perception that the international focus on ISIL has given it the upper hand. The United States government must continue its public rhetoric to clearly articulate how our efforts against ISIL do not supersede or somehow obviate the enduring U.S. policy goal of a transition from the Assad regime.

Third, to put pressure on the regime, and to ensure that the areas where ISIL is defeated do not fall into the hands of regime proxies, we must quickly and effectively train and assist moderate opposition units. The train and equip program newly authorized in the Fiscal Year 2015 National Defense Authorization Act should be implemented with a consideration for how and where these units will be re-inserted into Syria.[13] They will be trained to fight ISIL, but their presence and their partnership with the United States and its allies, including Saudi Arabia and Turkey, should also deter the regime and its proxies. Despite previous challenges to this end, the Department of State should complement the Department of Defense's new program with a renewed effort to help the Syrian opposition develop a credible and realistic political program envisioning a multi-sectarian, pluralistic post-transition governance plan with clear guarantees to Syrian minorities.[14]

Fighting ISIL in the Global Commons

Finally, we must combat ISIL in a global context. Here, U.S. military power should be used only sparingly, and only in situations where there is evidence of imminent plots by ISIL itself targeting the U.S. homeland. In the global theater, U.S. leadership will be critically important, particularly in support of four objectives:

First, the United States has significantly improved homeland security efforts and targeted them to the particular threat of foreign fighters with Western passports training and fighting with ISIL. Working with state and local authorities to counter sources of potential radicalization at home is a critical part of this effort.[15] In September, the United States introduced a Security Council resolution calling on all member states to stem the flow of foreign fighters to Syria and Iraq.[16] In part due to U.S. pressure and diplomatic support, members of the anti-ISIL Coalition are increasingly criminalizing foreign fighter-related activities and breaking up foreign fighter networks. Saudi Arabia has now issued formal decrees criminalizing ISIL and has broken up ISIL cells with links to Syria.

---

[13] Managing the degree to which Syrian rebel groups that are trained and equipped by the United States and its allies cooperate with organizations such as Jabhat al-Nusra that want to see Syria ruled as a sharia state in post-Assad order, will be a particular challenge to U.S. strategy in Syria.

[14] Dafna H. Rand and Nicholas A. Heras. "How This Ends: A Blueprint for De-Escalation in Syria," (Center for a New American Security, November 2014), 5.

[15] "A New Approach to Countering Violent Extremism: Sharing Expertise and Empowering Local Communities," FBI Law Enforcement Bulletin, October 7, 2014, http://leb.fbi.gov/2014/october/a-new-approach-to-countering-violent-extremism-sharing-expertise-and-empowering-local-communities; Anthony Vassalo and Dafna H. Rand, "Brining the Fight Back Home: Western Foreign Fighters in Iraq and Syria," Center for a New American Security, August 25, 2014, 8.

[16] "Security Council Unanimously Adopts Resolution Condemning Violent Extremism, Underscoring Need to Prevent Travel, Support for Foreign Terrorist Fighters," United Nations, September 24, 2014, http://www.un.org/press/en/2014/sc11580.doc.htm.

Second, counter-financing efforts remain a critical way to limit ISIL's capacity. The Coalition has made limited progress in destroying ISIL's refining capacity, denying ISIL its main source of revenue from the oil trade. Such efforts must be continued and expanded.

Third, while much has been done, far more is needed to address the toll of the region's conflicts on its civilians. The United States provided over $208 million for the humanitarian response in Iraq in Fiscal Year 2014, and has provided $3 billion for Syria in support of the UN-led humanitarian response since the start of the conflict in 2011. To date, the United States remains the largest single donor country helping to alleviate the Syrian humanitarian crisis; Coalition allies must match our humanitarian commitments.

Finally, ongoing U.S. and allied counter-messaging efforts seek to rebut ISIL's messages aggressively and in real time. It is promising that top religious leaders in Egypt and Saudi Arabia have issued fatwas declaring ISIL a direct threat to Islam. The United States should continue offering technical assistance to partners involved in implementing counter-messaging efforts, including by helping them to combat ISIL's social media presence.

Conclusion

In all three theaters, creative diplomacy, including efforts that sustain and lock-in the efforts of our partners, will be required to defeat ISIL over the medium term. Even as it deliberates the proper limitation on the authorization for military force against ISIL, Congress must also support and encourage these diplomatic efforts, including by ensuring that the U.S. government has sufficient resources to focus on the above priorities.

Chairman ROYCE. Thank you, Dr. Rand.

To get to a real world example, Ambassador Jeffrey, you raised the question. So ISIL has taken Mosul, and who is going to dig them out of there?

And this committee raised the issue before they got to Mosul that we should have used air power while they were on the open desert to decimate that force. But that wasn't done at that time.

So as of this morning, the peshmerga forces had surrounded ISIS in Mosul on three sides. They are working to cut ISIS' ability to maneuver in the area.

The greatest problem right now is the area south of Mosul where Iraqi Government forces and where the Sunni tribes are struggling to gain control of Saladin Province.

So when we look at the authorization just sent down to the committee, we are the committee of jurisdiction, so from the White House they sent to Congress an authorization that would provide the flexibility to conduct ground combat operations in limited circumstances and we go through some of the lists, the use of special operations forces to take military action against ISIL leadership and for intelligence collection and sharing and missions to enable kinetic strikes, in other words, on the ground in order to call in air strikes, and I guess there's about 3,000 special forces involved in that right now, or the provision of operational planning and other forms of advice and assistance of partner forces. I want to get to this question of assistance for our partner forces because I am concerned about the situation that the Kurds face.

We have had numerous meetings with them in which they have called repeatedly for anti-tank weapons that they could use, for artillery, for long-range mortar, you know, armor, and that has not been done.

And so as they surround Mosul this gets to the question of what kind of leadership on the ground would be given, what kind of weaponry would be given and what kinds of air strikes will be, you know, called in by our spotters on the ground.

And maybe we can open with that, Ambassador. Would you like to give us your thoughts on some of this?

Ambassador JEFFREY. Certainly, Mr. Chairman.

It is, to some degree, two separate questions. Arming the Kurds is an important issue and there are two elements to it.

One is what they need and, secondly, the political ramifications in the longer term because there will be an Iraq and there will be a lot of problems in the Middle East after we defeat ISIS, and one of the problems is keeping Iraq together.

So the administration's position—and it makes sense, it was the position we had when I was there—is to give these weapons through the Iraqi Government at least with a pro forma check to the Kurds.

We just have to try a lot harder to ensure that weapons go to the Kurds. It is easier for what I call defensive weapons.

These are MRAP and Humvee armored vehicles that are basically for counter insurgency. These would be anti-mine equipment, night vision goggles, armor and all of that thing.

The question is long-range artillery, as you mentioned, and armor because that can not only be used in an urban situation against ISIS, it can also be used in a conflict with Baghdad.

That is a tricky question. For the moment, I would focus on giving them better equipment to do what they are doing now to ensure that they have the ammunition, that they have the armor to move around the battlefield.

I am not sure that giving them artillery and tanks is such a good idea. Assuming they can hold their ground now, and they have been, including in a quite difficult attack in Kirkuk last week, in terms of the Kurds—the Peshmerga taking Mosul—there are various opinions on that.

Part of Mosul was always considered Kurdish in the sense that there was a Kurdish element to the population in east Mosul, and they may be willing to fight in or near that. I am not so sure they would be willing to take heavy casualties, and they would take heavy casualties to fight to take over——

Chairman ROYCE. Look, they are taking heavy casualties now. They are taking it against artillery when they don't have artillery to match. Only 25 of the 250 MRAPs that we sent through Baghdad got through.

So I am just—I am just pointing out that the weaponry is not getting through to the Kurds and I think on both sides of the aisle here—you know, the fighting is going to be done by Kurdish, by Jordanian, by Sunni tribes, by, you know, Arab troops and Kurdish troops on the ground.

And if we are not giving them the assistance they need, you know, this allows ISIS not to be rolled back. We need to see them decisively rolled back.

But let me go to Dr. Brennan just for a minute in terms of some of your thoughts on this because I know that you have written about peshmerga and coalition ground forces, the necessity to help them on the ground. Would you like to elaborate?

Mr. BRENNAN. Thank you—thank you, Mr. Chairman.

My view is that in order to assist these organizations, whether they be the peshmerga or coalition forces that we bring on the ground, we have got to put U.S. forces with them.

And that is the perfect mission that we have—the United States Army special forces. I would be putting A teams down at the battalion level to help them plan, get intelligence, to help them organize and to allow them to bring in the type of air support that is necessary at the precision level.

The problem that you are going to have as you go into cities is there will be a great reluctance to use air support as you are in there because of the potential for collateral damage.

Having our troops on the ground gives the sense of confidence that you can then bring those weapons where they are needed, and I think without having putting our boots on the ground to do that will be extremely difficult to win this battle.

Chairman ROYCE. We have about 3,000 special forces now, U.S. personnel, on the ground in theater and they are calling in air strikes right now. You are saying as you get into these cities they need to be forward deployed in order to make certain that the ISIL targets are the targets that are hit.

Mr. BRENNAN. Exactly, and they need to be engaged with all the coalition military so we have an integrated air campaign, an enhanced air campaign much greater than we have right now.

Chairman ROYCE. My time has expired.

I will go to Mr. Engel, the ranking member of the Foreign Affairs Committee.

Mr. ENGEL. Thank you very much, Mr. Chairman, and thank— I want to thank our witnesses for their testimony. Our hearing today takes place in the wake of President Obama sending his request for the use of force to the Congress yesterday.

The AUMF lands squarely in the jurisdiction of this committee and I look forward to working with Chairman Royce and all of our colleagues on both sides of the aisle to thoroughly review the President's proposal and our overall strategy to defeat ISIS in the days and weeks ahead.

We are, obviously, trying to deal with the appalling humanitarian situation including the 3 million Syrians and hundreds of thousands of Iraqis who have been driven from their homes as well as the spillover effect in Jordan, Turkey, Lebanon and Egypt.

We have worked to cut of ISIS' funding stream, cracking down on their efforts to smuggle oil and kidnap for ransom, and I am working on legislation to provide cultural properties so that groups like ISIS cannot steal a country's heritage and sell it to pay for the weapons of terror.

We are attempting to stem the flow of foreign fighters, helping to ensure that when we remove an ISIS extremist from the battlefield there isn't another recruit from France or England or the U.S. waiting to take his place, and the coalition is pushing back against false, dangerous and violent ideology preached in ISIS propaganda.

Coalition military operations are making some progress and under the cover of coalition air strikes we are seeing some reversals in ISIS gains.

As the chairman spoke about, we continue to advise and assist the Iraqi security forces and the Kurdish peshmerga, and I share the chairman's thoughts on the peshmerga and the Kurds.

Isis has been driven out of Kobani and we continue to prepare for training and equipping moderate vetted Syrian opposition, though this effort is slow moving and long, long, long overdue, in my opinion.

So the coalition is working on a multilateral, the way a multilateral effort should and when questions arise we are trying to meet concerns.

We are able to bring the UAE back into this effort as one of our most reliable allies in the region and that is why Jordan has doubled down on the commitment—on its commitment after the aftermath of the horrific murder of Captain al-Kasasbeh. Obviously, we are not out of the woods.

I want to start by talking about the AUMF. The President put his language as a starting point on the AUMF so I would like to hear from our witnesses what their thoughts are.

Should this AUMF be limited to a certain geographic area? Should it limit U.S. combat troops on the ground? Should we consider a sunset clause for an AUMF? Why don't we start with Ambassador Jeffrey?

Ambassador JEFFREY. I would urge the committee to give as much latitude as possible to the administration, particularly on timing. I am very concerned about the 3 years because having been in the administration it is going to be very difficult.

As they come in—the next administration comes into office and they are just getting their people confirmed in May or June 2017, to have to think about a resolution while also thinking about what their overall strategy is going to be—if there has to be a time limit on it, and I understand why people would want it, I would urge a broader one.

I am also a bit concerned about the enduring offensive ground operations because that can be interpreted to mean no ground operations.

Certainly, the kind of operations by special forces advisory teams and such that Dr. Brennan has talked about are very feasible and are the normal procedure in such campaigns—we have used them many times before—and if the commanders on the ground need them I think they should.

I would not rule out using American ground troops to take territory if that is necessary to defeat ISIS. What I would rule out myself, but that is a political decision, is long-term American presence on the ground as we saw in Iraq, in Afghanistan, in Vietnam. It does not work, Mr. Engel.

Mr. ENGEL. Isn't enduring—people on the other side worry that enduring might be allowing troops for a longer period of time than people would like? So you have got people on both sides of the divide worrying about the nebulous term enduring.

Ambassador JEFFREY. It is a bad idea to have enduring ground troop presence almost anywhere in the Middle East and we have traditionally not done that before 2001, 2003 and that's a good rule to get back to generally, with exceptions.

Advisory teams, air power, perhaps, in the long term but you don't want to keep a large ground presence because that is perceived as a threat by various actors in the region.

Mr. ENGEL. Thank you. Let me ask Dr. Brennan and then Dr. Rand to comment.

Mr. BRENNAN. I would agree with what Ambassador Jeffrey said. The other point I would like to make, though, is that limiting the President of the United States to—not allowing him to have enduring ground operations sends a signal not only to our friends but also to our enemies.

We have to go into this—if this is a grave threat to U.S. national security, I believe the Congress ought to authorize the President to do what is necessary and, more importantly, while there may be no plans to do an enduring operation, we do not know where the war is going to evolve in 6 months and we have to be able to have the flexibility of the President and commanders on the ground.

And I see this as somebody who has been with troops on the ground to say that the lawyers are going to be wrestling with this every day, trying to understand what is an enduring offensive operation or is it defensive, it is going to cause so many problems, that I think that it would be a mistake to keep a clause like this in the AUMF.

Mr. ENGEL. Thank you. Dr. Rand, you said a lot about this in your written testimony.

Ms. RAND. Overall, I think the AUMF strikes the right tone in terms of balancing between the flexibility requirement and reflecting the strategy, as I mentioned, that is working in a preliminary way.

The most important clause here, I think, is the sunset provision because, as my colleagues have mentioned, so much is changing and is fluid on the battlefield that the question of how extensive the ground forces need to be, the question of the geography, the question of what is an affiliate or associate of ISIS—these are questions that in 2 years, 3 years we will have to reevaluate.

Congress and the executive branch will have to reevaluate. So I see that, some type of prevention, as the most important limitation on the use of force because it demands a reevaluation of the strategy and demands questions such as metrics of success and progress that Congress will require based on reporting requirements in here.

The only final question I would add is the geographical scope in terms of the global—the global authorization for the use of force against ISIS' affiliates and associates. That might need to be clarified.

Mr. ENGEL. Thank you. Thank you, Mr. Chairman.

Chairman ROYCE. We go now to Ileana Ros-Lehtinen of Florida.

Ms. ROS-LEHTINEN. Thank you very much, Mr. Chairman.

The Obama administration states that the training of Syrian moderate fighters is a large part of our strategy. But as of yet, we have not seen much evidence of this success.

Former Ambassador to Syria Robert Ford said in our Middle East Subcommittee that the administration doesn't bother to coordinate or discuss strategy with Syria's moderate fighters at all and won't strike ISIL near Aleppo, the moderate stronghold.

If this force does eventually get up and running, what should its mission be and who will—who do you think will set and coordinate the strategy? Will it be the United States or the coalition partners?

Can these forces fight against Assad and ISIL simultaneously? And, Ambassador Jeffrey, you testified that Iran's policies almost drove Iraq apart between 2012 and 2014 and also that we won't be able to defeat ISIL over the long term without a more forceful U.S. policy toward the Assad regime.

What can you tell us about Iran's goal and the activities in Iraq and the region and how does this impact our fight against ISIL?

Do you suspect that we are not going after Assad because we are negotiating with Iran on nukes? And, lastly, when Iran violates Iraqi airspace, did or will Prime Minister Abadi, the U.S. and our coalition turn a blind eye because it is not convenient?

Ambassador JEFFREY. Thank you, Madam Chairman.

First of all, I agree with you that we need to do much more to explain how Syria fits in to this whole equation. The campaign is correct in putting the priority on Iraq because there we do have allies.

There we do have—we are engaged and Syria is a longer term question. But that doesn't mean you can now not answer questions. Our allies in the region—most of them want us to do more against

Assad. Assad contributed to the creation of ISIS. Assad is allied with Iran.

As my colleague Dr. Brennan said, we are dealing not just with one extreme Islamic violent movement in the region with ISIS. We are dealing with a whole series of them and one of them is the Wilayat al Faqih side of the Iranian establishment—the religious establishment.

It is both a country and a cause, and the poster boy for the cause is Qasem Soleimani, who has done a great deal to drive Iraq into the disunity that ISIS was able to exploit in 2014 by allowing and in some cases encouraging Maliki and other members of the Shi'a governing coalition to oppress the Sunnis and disagree with the Kurds such that the country was not holding together very well, and then ISIS came on the scene and we saw what happened. So we have to simultaneously deal with all of these problems.

We have a lot of friends in the region. I can't say that the administration doesn't do more against Iran or even Syria because of the negotiations. I hope that isn't the case. But I think that we need to separate the two out.

That negotiation on nuclear weapons has to rest on its own merits, whatever they may be, and our policy toward providing security in this region with our allies has to be moved forward without consideration of other exterior questions.

Ms. Ros-Lehtinen. Thank you so much. The other witnesses?

Mr. Brennan. We need to approach this issue from a regional—develop a regional strategy to address this. As Ambassador Jeffrey said, we have got a lot of partners in the region that are being threatened by what has taken place.

If you look at the rapid expansion of what Iran has done recently, currently they have—Hezbollah in Lebanon they have the large number of Shi'a militias in Iraq, perhaps as many as 5,000 to 10,000, and when we look at the success in Iraq, a lot of the success is being done by the Shi'a-led militias and Qasem Soleimani in Iran inside Iraq that will tend to distort Iraqi politics in the long run.

You have got the Houthi in Yemen and you have got Assad in Syria. You essentially have the creation of a Shi'a crescent that is threatening all of our allies in the region and it is no wonder that these allies, when we ask them to join us, come to us and are concerned because they see Iran as a primary threat.

And we have to come together and develop a strategy that takes consideration of our allies' concerns and moves on from there rather than just trying to look at, solely, at the issue of ISIS, although I agree with Ambassador Jeffrey——

Ms. Ros-Lehtinen. Thank you.

Mr. Brennan [continuing]. ISIS in Iraq has got to be the first priority.

Ms. Ros-Lehtinen. Thank you. Sorry I ran out of time. Thank you.

Chairman Royce. The ranking member of the Subcommittee on Terrorism here, Mr. Brad Sherman of California.

Mr. Sherman. Mr. Chairman, I have now become the ranking member on Asia but——

Chairman Royce. Congratulations on the promotion.

Mr. SHERMAN. For purposes—but I believe ISIS is a lesser threat to the United States than the Shi'ite alliance. Ground troops, if necessary to take territory, will be necessary to hold the territory. The peshmerga are not going to be welcomed in Sunni Arab areas and the Iraqi army, we saw what they did.

It was the greatest transfer of weaponry to a terrorist organization in history. The Shi'ite—the Iraqi Government has some effective fighting units. They are the Shi'ite militias that have engaged in murderous ethnic cleansing of Sunnis under reported in the American press and so it is—so I don't see who we have that will be a ground force to take Sunni areas.

I do know that I don't want to vote to have American soldiers going house to house in Mosul in a bloody hand to hand combat role because no other ground forces are available.

As to the AUMF, we have got the text the President sent over leaves in place the 2001 AUMF—in effect, republishes, reaffirms it. Well, what is that that we would be reaffirming 15 years later?

Unlimited in time, unlimited in what weapons or tactics or ground forces. It authorized over 100,000 forces—soldiers in Afghanistan. Last decade it would authorize 100,000 U.S. soldiers to be deployed on the ground next decade and, of course, unlimited in geography.

So if we republish rather than repeal that, it is hard to say that the President doesn't have enough authority to do all the things that many of us hope he does not do. And then as to the timing issue, it would—if Congress is doing its job and there's a 3-year AUMF, after 2 years we passed something else rather than waiting for 2 days while we have soldiers in the field wondering whether Congress will pass the bill.

But I want to focus with my time on economics. This is the richest terrorist organization in history. They got a huge quantity of Iraqi currency. I don't know if our witnesses have qualifications to focus on this.

What some countries have done is they have done currency exchanges. Your—you know, your blue money is going to be void because you got to change it for purple money.

This inconveniences the corrupt, tax evaders, et cetera, and therefore is extremely unpopular with governments that are dominated by corrupt tax evaders, which may very well describe Baghdad.

Do any of you—are any of you qualified to talk about whether Iraq should do a currently exchange designed to invalidate the many billions of dollars' worth of Iraqi currently that ISIS seized in the Mosul Bank? Well, we will move on to another question.

Chairman ROYCE. For what it is worth, Ranking Member, I think it is a—I think it is a good idea and I would suggest maybe after you reflect on it if you could have a written response to the congressman's question that would be helpful.

Mr. SHERMAN. Yes. And let me establish just a policy for this committee. I will yield automatically to any member who wants to say, "I have a good idea."

Chairman ROYCE. So it won't happen all the time.

Mr. SHERMAN. It is unlikely to interrupt me very often. In World War II, the French lived under enemy occupation and we regarded those areas as areas to be bombed and constricted. Obviously, you couldn't—the Vichy government wasn't allowed to buy Argentine wheat and just bring it in a ship across the ocean.

We regarded occupied France as an asset of the Nazis. Yet, I am told and news reports indicate that the Iraqi Government is paying the civil servants in Mosul and, of course, ISIS then takes as much of that money as they want. Do any of you have a comment about that and whether it should continue? Ambassador.

Ambassador JEFFREY. Certainly, Mr. Sherman, that is a tough question. I know that the Embassy is focused on that. They saw the news reports as well. It gets also to the question of can you just change the currency.

We did that from time to time in Vietnam. It had—when I was there—it had a lot of second and tertiary level impact on a lot of people. I think that the reason that the Iraqi Government is continuing these payments is, first of all, you know, it is hard to explain this but it is their legal obligations of the government to their civil servants. The second thing is that——

Mr. SHERMAN. Somehow the government in exile of France did not feel it necessary to pay the teachers of Vichy. Go on.

Ambassador JEFFREY. Right, but the government in exile in France was not considered the legal Government of France, deGaulle including, by us. That is a whole other complicated question.

The Iraqi Government is, and I think that is important, but the most important thing is it gets to the questions you have asked about who is going to do the liberating.

The answer is much of it by the Sunni population, the Sunni tribes, the Sunni members of those communities. They need to feel a certain loyalty to Baghdad. I am not so sure cutting off their money is going to give them that loyalty.

Mr. SHERMAN. Every penny that goes to ISIS-controlled areas is scooped up by ISIS. But just take 30 seconds to say in addition there are news reports that we are providing free electricity—the Iraqi Government provides free electricity to the ISIS areas.

So in World War II where we took it seriously we bombed the electric generation facilities in occupied France. Here, the Mosul Dam, I believe, provides electricity to Mosul. The Mosul Dam was retaken by Iraqi forces.

So it is not—it is not free electricity because the consumer has to pay. They pay ISIS. I yield back.

Chairman ROYCE. Thank you. We go now to Mr. Smith of New Jersey, chairman of the Subcommittee on Africa and Human Rights.

Mr. SMITH. Thank you very much, Mr. Chairman, for convening this important hearing.

I want to thank our three panelists for their extraordinary service to our country and providing this committee and by extension the American people the benefit of your insights and recommendations.

Ambassador Jeffrey, if I could ask you, you say you do not think a campaign of strategic patience is appropriate. How do you think President Obama defines that?

You also point out that—in your testimony that the stress when the coalition begins a major ground offensive operations would occur.

You talked about day-after scenarios and a containment mission that would eventually—would eventually crater the coalition to lead to new ISIS threats and then you say time is not on our side and that the administration has to move faster.

Has the administration moved fast enough years to date and does the President's AUMF meet the criteria to move faster?

Ambassador JEFFREY. Thank you very much, Mr. Chairman.

First of all, the administration moved not at all after my colleague, Brett McGurk, came up here and talked to you over a year ago and that has led to a tragedy—first, Fallujah in January and then Mosul in June.

I will say, as having worked with this administration, that I am surprised at how rapidly the administration responded in August when Erbil was threatened, and since then I think that the administration and the Central Command has done a very good job putting together this coalition, getting a lot of steel on target and stopping and in some cases pushing back ISIS.

My problem is more what is going to happen next. This gets to the question of strategic patience. President Obama has laid this out last week in his national security strategy.

He laid it out in his interview with CNN's Fareed Zakaria and he laid it out in his State of the Union speech. The President is, clearly, very nervous about the use of military force, particularly ground forces, without a lot of allies, without a lot of legal backing, without the support of you and everybody else.

Sometimes that is necessary. Sometimes that is smart. We could have used a little bit more of that a decade ago. But there are times when action is necessary. I am concerned we may not be moving fast enough.

Mr. SMITH. Could I just ask you as well how do you think ISIS—the ISIS leadership and other interests who are completely antithetical to our interests in the region look at what is happening at the White House and what is happening up here?

Ambassador JEFFREY. That is a very good point, and I was about to use it saying any restrictions on the authorization is going to encourage the enemy—don't encourage the enemy. But fear is fear.

These guys are so busy dodging precision munitions right now that I don't think they are going to spend a lot of time. What I worry about is Iran, Russia, China.

In all of our conversations, members of this committee, that we talk about with ISIS we have to take this in the context of a whole extraordinary variety of challenges we have seen over the last year.

China, Russia, al-Qaeda elements on the march, particularly in North Africa, ISIS itself, Syria and Iran—they are all watching us. ISIS probably won't respond the most to any signs of weakness but others might, and I am concerned across the board with all of these challenges.

Mr. SMITH. With all due respect to the administration, I have repeatedly asked that they designate Boko Haram a foreign terrorist organization. We had several hearings on it. Finally, I introduced legislation.

On the day when we were having another hearing after visits by myself and others to both Jos and Abujah, we were getting ready to mark up the bill. The administration announced it a day late and a dollar short but welcomed it nevertheless.

The parallels to Boko Haram—if we don't train, in my opinion, and secure the cooperation of the Nigerian military, I was in Jos. I saw how they had firebombed so many churches.

They are going after Christians with a vengeance but they are also going after Muslims who stand in their way. Your thoughts on the parallels—again, what we do vis-à-vis ISIS as well as training up battalions who are human rights vetted Nigerian soldiers to combat Boko Haram.

Ambassador JEFFREY. Again, and I would go back to some of my responses I made earlier and perhaps modify them on the peshmerga, basically, you have to find allies who are willing to fight.

If they are willing to fight, I wouldn't worry all that much about vetting them. I would give them weapons. In the case of Iraq, it is a bit complicated but—and it is very complicated about sending the peshmerga into certain areas. But, certainly, they deserve more support from us.

They are doing well and I hope they get it. People who are fighting Boko Haram deserve support from us, the same kind of support that we are giving the folks in Iraq.

This is a region wide struggle with a many-headed enemy and I think that if you are a day short and a dollar behind and only at the last minute you take action such as declare Boko Haram, obviously, a terrorist organization you have just defined strategic patience.

Mr. SMITH. Again, thank you for your testimony and for your leadership.

Chairman ROYCE. Mr. Meeks of New York, ranking member of the Subcommittee on Europe.

Mr. MEEKS. Thank you, Mr. Chairman, and I want to thank the witnesses for your testimony today.

I look at these hearings as I did back in 2001 when we were endeavoring to try to decide what was the best thing to do there and I also try to utilize where we are now, understanding what took place in 2001 and so that we could have learned from it.

And sometimes I think what the President is talking about when you say patience, et cetera, we didn't have any patience. In fact, we thought that and sometimes we think that it is a quick hit.

I remember very well when Shock and Awe happened, and then a few days later we saw the President of the United States say mission accomplished. We thought that that was going to be it.

Many members of this committee said once we got in there that individuals will be waving a flag and saying, thank you, America and we are bringing all of our values to them and they would just embrace it and that would be the great thing and everything would be different. Ten, eleven years later, we still had troops on the ground, are still there.

We committed—we have committed more in the region than anyone else and still yet I hear folks say we didn't do—no one has lost over 6,000 lives in military combat.

It is us, and then I still hear and I have heard some testimony here today where our allies said, well, you, United States, you need to get back out there and get some more folks. Yet, in their region they are the ones that are the immediately threat.

We are going to help our allies because they are in our strategic interests. But the ones that are in immediate danger are those that are right around there. So we need to back out and say, look, you all got to do something, too.

We are losing our lives. We put our lives on the line. We are ready to give you all the strategic help that you can get and I think that we should.

The President was very clear—keep our special ops—and if we find that there is somebody over there from ISIL, that their organization and some of our allies cannot get to them, well, that is when we want to use that limited number that is in the AUMF so that they can go after those guys and absolutely destroy them.

And I do think, you know, clearly, and I think that became more evident than ever that this is not a malicious group because if you see what they did to the Jordanian pilot that is so anti-Islam and if you see how they are acting that is so anti-Islam.

These are thugs and terrorists, and so we have got to make sure that is out there with reference to delegitimizing their ideology and I think, you know, someone else said well, you know, they are—what they are doing with their PR folks maybe, you know, they are just asking us to come in.

They want to us—because I think they do because they would love for us to have people on the ground on a continuous basis. Why? That is their best recruitment.

If it was us on the ground and they can recruit more folks to fight against us because then they can say it is them against us and that is why we have got to resist that temptation because otherwise when people start to—we start to delegitimize their ideology then their recruitment will begin to rescind.

Now, I happen to agree and I think, Dr. Rand, with your testimony because I think we have got to do a whole lot of things on a multilateral basis—diplomacy, you know, some military, some this—and it is not all about and mostly what I am hearing is military. We have got to do some other things.

So let me just ask this question because I did agree with Dr. Rand in her opening statement. Ambassador Jeffrey, what was wrong with Dr. Rand's testimony this morning?

Ambassador JEFFREY. Nothing at all. It was really good testimony and I agree with it. What I would say is, again, if we are getting back to strategic patience, if strategic patience means not making the mistakes of the last decade, I will sign up to strategic patience.

If strategic patience, however, means—and it is not only this administration who has looked at it this way—that it means no casualties and no risk of casualties it means assuming that the people in the region not only have more at stake than us—that is a debatable thing—but assuming that they can carry a big part of the burden I don't see anything in our history.

At the beginning of this meeting or hearing, Chairman Royce talked about us doing 85 percent of the strikes, I believe.

I would say if you look at Libya 4 years ago, if you look at Bosnia, if you look at Kosovo where we had all of NATO, you will find—if you look at the Korean War other than the Koreans themselves you will find similar statistics for the last 70 years.

We can complain about that but that is how we have maintained international security. Where we have run into trouble and three times going into North Korean, Vietnam and Iraq have been, as you pointed out, we thought that we could do regime change and we could change populations.

We are not going to do that but I don't think anybody up here today is suggesting that. What we are suggesting or at least two of us are that we be—at least consider if our military commanders and if our diplomats need it a more aggressive policy militarily but, as I said, a more aggressive set of diplomatic actions.

Mr. MEEKS. Let me just—Dr. Rand, what do you have to say?

Ms. RAND. Sure. Just to clarify the testimony in my opening statement, I am not advocating for a more aggressive use of force than has been suggested by the AUMF text.

I also look at the lessons learned from the past 10 years and the fight, particularly in Iraq. This is the 25th year that the U.S. is involved in some military combat operation in Iraq if you think about it—if you count all the operations in the 1990s.

And so it is quite remarkable that we are still talking about Iraq and we are still talking about the proper use of American force. There are two lessons learned, and I would agree with you, Congressman.

The first one, in my mind, is don't make Americans part of the story. You know, you are not leading from behind. You are not taking a back seat role.

But you don't want to insert our presence to change the dynamic and create an insurgency against American power. That was clear in the 2003–2004 situation.

The second, and my colleagues have alluded to it, is the importance of the ISF being sustainable or the ISF peshmerga—most of the ISF—the Iraqi Government and security forces need to be multi sectarian, professional and less susceptible to the penetration by outside actors like Iran, like the Shi'ite militias.

That is the only way to sustain and protect Iraq as a sovereign country over the long term. You know, we have had the Sons of Iraq, the awakening.

We have had problems with the Sunni region and its connectivity with central Baghdad. This is the second time, third time this has happened and so we need to create a force that will really think of itself as representing the security of all Iraqis and that will take time and that is part of the strategic issues.

And that is what the trainers are doing, by the way, and it is better and more effective to train them with our Arab allies, which is what we are doing, and our European allies all over Iraq right now. We are training 12 new brigades, as you know. Thank you.

Chairman ROYCE. Thank you. We go now to Mr. Rohrabacher of California, chairman of the Subcommittee on Europe, Eurasia, and Emerging Threats.

Mr. ROHRABACHER. Thank you very much, Mr. Chairman, and I want to thank the witnesses for coming here. We have—this is a discussion between us and the witnesses about what direction we should go and we appreciate your advice.

Dr. Brennan, let me just note that I agree with your basic assessment that we are not just talking about ISIL or ISIS, whatever—which one we want to call it—that this actually is an enemy that has been 10 years or 15 years around us and its radical Islamic fanatic terrorism or groups that are willing to use terrorism to terrorize the Western world and this goes back all the way to even before 9/11 when we lost 3,000 Americans, murdered, to try to terrorize our country.

So these groups, whether we call them ISIL or whether they are burning somebody to death there to try to say—show us how mean and nasty they are or whether they are trying to bring down buildings in New York, it is that—is the same enemy whether those—whatever they want to call their organization at whatever particular moment.

So with this I would suggest that that is the primary threat that we face in the Western world faces today. That is our primary threat to our security and our safety and the United States needs to recognize that and figure out how we defeat these type of enemies.

Let me just note that I personally will not and I don't—I can't speak for my colleagues but I don't believe that I will be giving the President of the United States and I don't think the Congress will give the President of the United States a blank check on the use of American military force in the Arab World or in the Gulf, wherever it is, and by the way it is maybe not specific enough, in the territory much less the timing of this.

We are not going to give him a blank check for a given period of time. We need to know exactly—if that means that he would be willing to commit major forces on the ground or not that needs to be part of any agreement that we have.

So I don't see this just, you know, being oh, the President is asking, thus he is going to get whatever he wants. We need to work it out—work out the details.

I personally don't believe this is going to be settled by the military. When we eliminated the Soviet Union, which was then the ultimate threat to peace and stability in the world, it was done by not by deployment of large numbers of troops and we need to create a dynamic that will end with the defeat of this threat to Western civilization.

We need to create that dynamic and that means what we did to defeat communism we made that our number-one goal and we worked with anybody who would work with us to defeat that goal and that made it, by the way, possible four us to defeat them without a conflict—direct military conflict with the United States.

Let me just note that I think this President has not reached out—we have already heard about the Kurds and to other people and other groups in the world and especially in that region who should be our best friends and mobilize them in this effort whether it is General Sisi or whether it is the people who are fighting against the—who marched against radical Islam in Tehran where the President couldn't get himself to say anything about that in support of those kids earlier on.

So we need to have that dynamic created rather than just having the President come to us and asking for military—for a military blank check, and the question I have—I know, I am—we are just about out of time here but let me just note this.

I would like to ask about shouldn't we be working with Assad? We worked with Stalin to defeat Hitler. We had all sorts of questionable allies when we were going against the Soviet Union.

Shouldn't we work with Assad? Shouldn't we be working with Putin in order to defeat this threat that you have capsulized for us of radical fanatic Islam? And that is my question to you, sir.

Ms. ROS-LEHTINEN. Thank you. The gentleman's time has expired.

Mr. ROHRABACHER. I ask unanimous consent that he be able to answer.

Ms. ROS-LEHTINEN. No objection.

Mr. BRENNAN. I think we need to be able to talk to all the countries in the region. But I think if you go back to my earlier argument, Assad is actually a part of this broader Islamist movement that is supported by Tehran.

So we have—we have in the Middle East today what is the equivalent of Sunni-Shi'a civil war that is taking place and at one level we need to determine which side of this we are on and how are we going to try to pull together these various countries in order to address the issue.

You are absolutely right. It is a radical Islamist ideology writ large, Sunni and Shi'a. We have to—but we need a grand strategy for it. Military is just one component of that.

But that is where we ought to be going and I think if there is one thing that comes out of this committee it could be a process of thinking about how do you move forward to confront this global threat to our interests, not just ISIS or one of the other groups.

Ms. ROS-LEHTINEN. Thank you, Mr. Rohrabacher.

Mr. Sires of New Jersey.

Mr. SIRES. Thank you, Madame Chair, and thank you very much for your service to the country and for being here.

You know, every time I sit here and I hear witnesses talk to me about training the Iraqi army, it just gives me the shivers because of the experiences that we have had with this idea of training.

I don't know where we get the confidence that if we train this army it is going to solve our problems because, you know, we have spent billions. When they took a shot at them then they ran.

So to go back and start training people again and spending all that money, you know, I am just concerned that at the end of all this people are going to say the only people that can solve the problem is us putting troops on the ground and I would never vote for that.

We lost 6,000 lives. We have countless people coming back. We have soldiers coming back committing suicide and for what? We solve one problem, one group—another one pops up. You know, I don't know the answer, obviously. You know, you are the experts. You know, I just take your word for it, you know, what you are saying.

But I do agree with you that we should fund the Kurds and we should give them the weapons that they need, and I am wondering where—a few years ago President Biden said that maybe Iraq should be divided in three—I wonder how viable that is. I mean, all these groups—maybe it is not viable now but just seemed like an idea back then.

And I am concerned about Jordan. You know, I am concerned about the impact that the refugees are having on the economy of Jordan and more and more people keep coming, and I am concerned are we doing enough to make sure that our friend, Jordan, is well prepared to deal with what they are dealing now.

I mean, they have taken a big step. They have stepped forward. So maybe you can just comment a little bit.

I don't know if some of the things that I may be wrong about. Training the Iraqis may be the only option but I got to tell you, it is hard for me to accept that.

Ambassador JEFFREY. Good questions, Mr. Chairman. The Iraqi troops ran in Mosul. The Iraqi army did not really run in Anbar Province.

Maliki pulled the troops out of Fallujah in January because of a political dispute and they rushed in and took over the police, who were in many cases much weaker than the military.

The military—they have had some bad days in Anbar Province but they haven't upped and ran. My experience in a good number of laws on various levels including out there trying to train them is that you can train forces to do well.

It helps a hell of a lot if you have American troops, advisory teams and American air power with them. The Vietnamese ran in 1972 when the North Vietnamese came in until we put in massive air strikes and we had our advisory teams out there fighting with them and the result was they turned the tide and pushed the North Vietnamese back.

I have seen this also in Iraq in 2010–2011. Iraqi troops did well against hard core al-Qaeda but particularly when they had American advisory teams with them.

So that is the first question. In terms of popping up, having been—spending much of my life since the 1974 Yom Kippur War where I was almost deployed to the region with a lot of other American troops I have a feeling of popping up too because it is what is—the history of my life over the last 40 years is constantly being redeployed to the Middle East in one or another capacity.

My take away from this is this is something we are not going to fix. We can provide multipliers to the people fixing it and the most important is assuring that really radical violent elements do not get a hold of large territories.

That is the Iranians, that is ISIS, that is al-Qaeda, that is Assad. And to contain and beat back those forces so that the people of the region have the chance to eventually move on the way people in the Balkans, the way people in Central America and the way people in other places where we have been successful have moved on.

But you are right. This is a long struggle and it is frustrating and because it is a long struggle we shouldn't tie a lot of troops down in a high casualty effort to fix this once and for all because we won't.

Mr. SIRES. How about Biden's idea then?

Ambassador JEFFREY. I am sorry. He has recanted, first of all, and secondly, the problem with that is I know of no border in the Middle East and, frankly, no border in any area I have ever been stationed in the Balkans or elsewhere that you can just break up into three parts because there are overlapping groups living in those areas.

There are overlapping historical memories and what these people will do is they won't agree to a piece of paper. They will fight, and it just creates evermore chaos. You change one border in the Middle East, they are all going to start being shaky and we will have yet another even bigger problem.

Mr. SIRES. Thank you. Thank you, Madame Chair.

Ms. ROS-LEHTINEN. Thank you very much, Mr. Sires.

And now we turn to Mr. Salmon, and our deepest condolences to all of the residents of Arizona for Kayla.

Mr. SALMON. Thank you very much. I really appreciate that.

I guess my question is to anyone on the panel that would like to take a stab. But, Ambassador, I would really appreciate your thoughts first on it.

Let me just say first, for the record, that I very much support a very robust AUMF being given to the President which gives maximum flexibility to our generals so that they can prosecute this effort until we win and we do it quickly—as quickly as possible.

But the President and his advisors have been clear for the last several months anyway that they believe that they have full legal authority under the 2001 AUMF to prosecute ISIL.

My question is why would the President be submitting to Congress or asking Congress to give him an AUMF that ties his hands. I have never heard of a President sending that kind of a request to Congress—please time my hands and give me a time limit and also, you know, limit my ability to use ground forces.

I get really frustrated. I marvel, in fact. I can't imagine Franklin Delano Roosevelt standing up before the American people and saying here is the five things I am not going to do to the Japanese.

It just doesn't make a lot of sense to telegraph what we are willing to do and what we are not willing to do and if the President believes that he has the authority, and I believe he has said that many times—some of his advisors—that he has the authority, why would he want a further limiting AUMF?

Ambassador JEFFREY. Very quickly, so my colleagues can—he does have the authority under the existing legislation but it is an awkward fit and he is absolutely right to come back here and ask for more specific from all of you.

In terms of why would he limit it, that is his philosophy and I have to be fair to him. I have worked for him. He doesn't think that military force can often be a solution and he thinks that we have gotten very committed, almost like a drug, to using military force rather than other means of national power.

I disagree with him but it is an honest position. He can point to areas from marching into North Korea to Vietnam to Iraq that I and others have cited where we have gone astray and it is something to really worry about.

But while I wouldn't support that position myself, I mean, I understand why he has it and a lot of Americans agree with him.

Mr. SALMON. Let me just modify that, Dr. Brennan, before you do speak. I also believe that one of the reasons for the conflicts that you cited that we were not very successful is that the politicians micro managed the whole damn thing. Dr. Brennan?

Mr. BRENNAN. I agree with Ambassador Jeffrey. We need to put something on the ground that is wide enough, that gives the President the ability to make the decision. He may choose he doesn't want to do that but—and that is a legitimate choice that he should make.

But I think that if the issue is as I portrayed in my testimony—I think as the others have, I think that this is a great threat to U.S. national security.

If it is a grave threat, as the President put in his AUMF, then we need to be giving the President everything that he needs and you don't know what is going to happen 6 months from now, and to have a complete going back and forth on this I think just ties his hands.

And I agree with you, Congressman, that I think that it makes most sense to look back and perhaps the 2001 AUMF could be cleaned up or amended to provide the types of capability that are needed.

It is not a perfect fit but whether or not we need to restrict the hands I would be very concerned about that as a commander as well as somebody who is trying to look about how the country moves forward on this.

Mr. SALMON. I am going to run out of time and I do have one other question because I am deeply concerned that the administration isn't very serious about this fight.

With only 250 coalition sorties flown a month versus the roughly 1,000 air strikes a day we flew in previous conflicts in the region, couldn't we do more with the air power that we have to at least degrade ISIL or ISIS and couldn't additional air power support further attack ISIS' impressive funding streams that they are using to support their caliphate?

Mr. BRENNAN. I believe that we ought to be putting—having a much more robust air campaign. But to do that you need to have more targetable intelligence and you get that kind of targetable intelligence by having troops out forward with our allies.

And without having that then I think that you run the risk of having collateral damage which will run counter to our policy, counter to our strategy and counter to the interests we have in Iraq.

Mr. SALMON. So it gets back to the ground forces and the support again?

Mr. BRENNAN. I believe so.

Ms. ROS-LEHTINEN. Thank you, Mr. Salmon.

Mr. Higgins of New York.

Mr. HIGGINS. Thank you, Madame Chair.

I just—you know, it amazes me in all of these hearings how quickly we just kind of bypass the fact that the United States paid about $25 billion to build up an Iraqi army and the first test of that army was against the Islamic State of Iraq and Syria, and they essentially ran.

And we were told that the reason that they were not committed to the fight was because the previous prime minister, Nouri al-Maliki, was not inclusive of the Shi'a-Sunni population and therefore didn't feel as though it was a fight worth committing to.

And now we are told that there is a new prime minister who is also a Shi'a but more inclusive of the Sunni community and therefore we should have confidence again in the Iraq national army.

Twenty-five billion dollars, thousands of lives lost and no commitment. Who are the most effective fighters in Iraq today?

The peshmerga—190,000—and the Shi'a militia. The new prime minister has said that there are about 1 million Shi'a militias who are trying to fill the void of the ineffectual Iraqi army.

Mr. Brennan, you had said earlier—you talked about the Shi'a militias who recently experienced success against ISIS. You also made reference to Qasem Soleimani, the Iranian Quds Force's leader who really negotiated the second term of Nouri al-Maliki with one condition—that the Americans leave—that the Americans leave.

And now we have a President who has a resolution before Congress asking for authorization to engage, again, militarily. You know, the Shi'a militias are not there to prop up the Iraqi Government.

They are there to do what Soleimani and others in asymmetrical warfare try to do and that is create a proxy in places that they want to control be it in southern Lebanon, be it in Syria or be it in Iraq.

My concern is that if we commit American forces, and there is no passive wing of the American military—everybody has weapons and everybody fights and they die courageously when they do—we are continuing a situation in this country that has been going on for way too long.

You know, Tom Friedman, the author and New York Times columnist, once said is Iraq the way it is because Saddam was the way he is, or is Saddam the way he is because Iraq is the way it is. And I think it just speaks again to the sectarian tribal nature of a place that we are trying to impose a political solution to.

You know, we are told that the American military with extraordinary courage, extraordinary commitment, extraordinary effectiveness, could only do one thing—create a breathing space within which the Shi'a, Sunni and Kurdish community could achieve political reconciliation including the sharing of oil revenues and we saw a hopeful sign in December that that was occurring between the central government in Baghdad and Kurdistan with the 17-percent sharing of the national revenues and also $1 billion to equip and train the peshmerga.

But I will tell you, where our investment has been made financially, where our investment has been made morally, has been an abject failure and what we are proposing to do with this resolution by the President is continue that failed policy without any clarity about what it is we are going to achieve because when there is no political center—here is what we know in that part of the world—when there is no political center there are only sides to choose and right now there is no political center.

And don't argue that the changing of a Shi'a prime minister in Iraq is going to fundamentally change the will and the commitment of the Iraqi national army.

You know, let us just acknowledge that our investment of $25 billion in the Iraqi national army failed—failed miserably—because when you say they all ran, 250,000 of them, in the face of 30,000 ISIS fighters, well, certainly because Iraq is a majority Shi'a country, many of those fighters would be Shi'a. So at least they wouldn't run.

So I don't know really what is going on here but I know where this is leading and I think most Americans know where this is leading, and it is not in a good place because, again, America is essentially going it alone for the third time in two different countries and unless there is a recognition of minority rights, unless there is a recognition of the pluralistic nature of Iraq, there will never be peace there and——

Ms. ROS-LEHTINEN. The gentleman's time has expired. Thank you, Mr. Higgins.

Mr. HIGGINS. Yield back. Thank you.

Ms. ROS-LEHTINEN. Mr. Issa of California.

Mr. ISSA. Thank you, Madam Chair. You know, being this far down the dais is of some help because a lot of—a lot of good questions have been asked.

One that I don't think really has been covered, because we are considering the authorization for use of military force, is sort of what we have and what we need, and let me just run through it quickly.

In 2001, the AUMF basically said global war on terror, al-Qaeda—go anywhere, get them. 2002, it was specifically Iraq—liberate Iraq. I think it is fair to say that whether we like the way Iraq is or not, it has been liberated.

Any new problem in Iraq very clearly is a new Iraq, and that is where I have some real challenges with the President's belief that he has any authority under the 2002. But leaving that aside, they are both obsolete.

Al-Qaeda, as we knew it, is no longer al-Qaeda as we knew it. Would I get your agreement that as we defined it in 2001 it is really a different organization? Is that fair to say?

And anything we do in Iraq and Syria and other areas in which derivative organizations including ISIL or Daesh is in fact at least fundamentally different or expanded and fits a slightly different definition. So we all agree on that part, I think.

So let me—let me ask the broader question. Aren't we dealing with two ideological groups, both of whom are a threat to regional security, to democracy and to the West, to a certain extent? One of them, Daesh, is a radicalized derivative of what we once knew as al-Qaeda.

The other, the Shi'a activist, whether it is Hezbollah, Tehran directly or various groups at any level, are ultimately a group that looks at the 12th Imam Mahdi—Muhammad Mahdi—and his proclamation of what you have to do which is more or less take the Holy Lands and bring back all the glory and peace.

And I listened to the former President of Iran at the U.N. in 2012 and he may be crazy but that is what he was saying is the

12th Imam is going to bring this all back and it was a call for jihad for the Shi'a.

Question, and I will start with Dr. Brennan but all of you can answer it, aren't we really dealing with the need to be targeted against both as appropriate and at the same time—and I will use Syria, an area that I have worked a little bit in, as the poster child—we have, if you will, the Mahdi 12th Imam crowd on one side backing Assad and then we have ISIL.

Aren't we in a position in which we have to make sure that we give a nimble authority to the President but one in which he weighs the comparative balances, one in which he clearly does no harm to one group, however reprehensible, that simply advances the other?

And isn't that really the Shi'a—and Doctor, this is why I want to go to you first—the Shi'a-Sunni conflict that we are now in the middle of? It is not just ISIL. It is not just Bashar Assad. It is not just Hezbollah.

We have metastasized into a conflict in which in many cases we are fighting on one side and empowering our enemy on the other side. Doctor?

Mr. BRENNAN. Congressman, I agree with your assessment on that. I think that as we are looking at the conflict between Sunni and Shi'a, we have to be—understand that this Islamist movement is a cancer that has evolved from—metastasized from various elements of Islam but it—and we need to go back and take a look at and reinforce those people who are really helping us.

King Abdullah has made some courageous stands. You look at King—President al-Sisi in Egypt. This has got to be done through them and we have to be working politically to encourage them and all of our neighbors, all those neighbors that have been our allies for the last 10 years, 20 years, 30 years.

So the Gulf States, Saudi Arabia—they need to change internally to stop what is going on but we can encourage them to do that.

Mr. ISSA. Okay. Let me narrow the question because I think you said it very well.

Isn't the President's obligation with whatever authority we give him to work with those who will be forces for moderation or at least tolerance in the region and you mentioned President al-Sisi who has been disrespected by this administration in an amazing way.

They were quick to recognize the Muslim Brotherhood and very slow to even call the President after he was legally elected in internationally recognized elections and, obviously, King Abdullah, as an example of a Sunni leader who is simply trying to bring back a moderate Sunni border to his near Jordan. But, quickly—I know my time has expired—this, for me, is the important part.

I don't want to topple a Syria that Iran has power in to get at ISIL but I don't want to defeat Sunni extremists only to empower a Shi'a aspiration paid for out of a dictatorial Iran that since 1975—1979 has consistently managed to ruin country after country and continues doing so. So please——

Ms. ROS-LEHTINEN. Thank you, Mr. Issa.

Mr. Cicilline.

Mr. CICILLINE. Thank you, Madam Chair. Thank you to the witnesses for your testimony and for your excellent written testimony as well. It was very helpful.

I want to just build for a moment on the gentleman from New York's last questions. One of the things I am very concerned about is that I don't think we have a clear understanding of what the end game is or what success even looks like and I think it builds on what you are saying, Dr. Brennan, that it is more than just defeating and killing individuals who are members of a terrorist organization but it is really do we have the ability to kill an ideology—a radical Islamist terrorist ideology.

So I think one of the things that I am struggling with is I have deep skepticism that continued or deepening military engagement is the solution and in fact real questions about whether it will in fact make it worse and more long term in part because of what you raised, Dr. Brennan, in your testimony.

But if you think about the role of the Iraqi security forces and you think about the money that we have spent and now we have embarked on a training of the Syrian opposition—the so-called moderate Syrian opposition—how can we have confidence that there will be any different result and over what period of time?

I mean, we are talking about beginning this training process now. Presumably, ISIS and ISIS fighters will not remain—you know, stand still while we sort of get up to speed.

So how should we tell the American people that we should have any confidence after having spent $25 billion and training hundreds of thousands of Iraqi soldiers that somehow this time it is going to be different, that they are going to take up the fight. So that is my first question.

My second question is that, you know, we talk a lot about the role of our international partners in this coalition and then we learn that 85 percent of the air strikes are by the U.S., and is it just impossible to imagine that the UAE and Saudi Arabia and Jordan and Egypt who are in the region will actually take on the responsibility, the chief responsibility, for this ground operation and for the air strikes?

Do they just not have the capacity? Do they not have the interest because of the political context? But, you know, everyone seems to suggest it is going to require air strikes and ground operations to be successful, whatever that means, but nobody seems to have identified who the ground troops are and we talk about peshmerga, which is great, and they are doing a terrific job.

But there are all these allies in the region who have real resources and real armies. Do they just—you know, I am interested in why they are not playing a greater role.

So those are my first two questions. I have one more but I want to be sure you have time to respond to those two.

Mr. BRENNAN. Just real quick on the last one you had. The reason the United States provides so much air support is because we have a capacity to do that.

The other allies in the region, Jordan being one of the more—the stronger ones—has capacity but it is limited and I think what they are doing now is probably as much as they can.

In terms of the ground forces, as the Ambassador commented earlier, each one of these countries has an Islamist problem in their own country and those armies that are there that they have are being used to maintain security in those countries.

So they can deploy some but they still need to maintain security within their own borders and so that is a challenge for them.

Ambassador JEFFREY. First of all, I have a lot of sympathy to what you have said because I have been out there and I have lived this. But it is not just in the Middle East.

Again, since World War II, we have had conflict after conflict where the number of Saudis, the number of infantry companies on the ground, have been somewhere between 50 and 90 percent American, where our allies often flee or leave behind their American equipment they were doing that, as I said, in June 1950 in South Korea and we have seen it ever since.

We have also seen though, including in Korea, including in Vietnam—I have seen it with my own eyes—including in Iraq, I have seen it with my own eyes, where they turn around and go back.

Often, we, including small numbers of we, can make and do make a difference. But there I will agree with Mr. Higgins. Particularly in the Middle East, in my 18 years counting Turkey that I served there I never felt one day that I was in a good place compared to even the rest of the world——

Mr. CICILLINE. Ambassador Jeffrey, I want to just give Dr. Rand a moment to also respond, please. Sorry to interrupt you.

Ms. RAND. I would just finally add that these are two excellent, excellent questions, Congressman, and I think the answers are actually linked, right. What is different about this enterprise right now is actually the partners that are involved.

So if you consider in November and the December the reformation of the Iraqi Government, these Arab neighbors were not at all interested in the formation of the Iraqi Government post-Saddam. They were not there. The Ambassador can attest to that.

They in fact were distancing themselves from Iraq. They sent no Ambassadors. They had no Embassies. It was really unprecedented in some way that all the neighbors were quite involved unanimously in helping Prime Minister Abadi get started and adding political capital and that is—to me, none of this is particularly promising but that is a source of promise that suggests to me that there could be a chance for this new Iraqi Government that will be different than the mistakes of its predecessors. Thank you.

Mr. CICILLINE. Thank you. I yield back.

Ms. ROS-LEHTINEN. Thank you, Mr. Cicilline.

Mr. Brooks of Alabama.

Mr. BROOKS. Thank you, Madam Chairman.

I want to follow up on some of the comments of my colleagues, David Cicilline of Rhode Island and Darrell Issa of California, and some of the responses plus some of the written testimony that we have had the benefit of.

Dr. Brennan stated in a response to a question from Darrell Issa that the Islamic State has "metastasized from various elements of Islam." Further, in Dr. Brennan's written testimony, I am going to read some quotes:

"While the threat is often portrayed as terrorism, the true danger is the ideology that provides the logic of extremism, violence and acts of inhumanity."

Next, another Dr. Brennan quote:

"While bin Laden has been killed, the ideology of Salafi jihadism continues to spread and the global threat posed by al-Qaeda, ISIS and affiliated groups is greater than ever."

Next, again, from Dr. Brennan:

"While the tactic of terrorism is frequently the immediate threat focused upon by political leaders, I think it is critical to note that the ideology underlying these actions seeks revolutionary change of the existing political and social order.

"Thus, the strategic challenge of our generation isn't one particular group of insurgents or terrorists. It is the ideology that gives them cause. Defeating this ideology will require the development of a grand strategy that employs all elements of national power and influence."

And then, finally, Dr. Rand—I am going to quote from her written remarks:

"ISIL's savage tactics are at the very core of its ideology. While al-Qaeda justifies individual suicide bombing attacks against civilians and civilian areas through fatwas explaining the conditional necessity, ISIL has adopted a new ideology, manipulating select stories from Islamic history and modern jihadi texts to redefine jihad and to generate a blanket justification for violence including against women and children."

If we take these remarks of Dr. Rand and Dr. Brennan on face value, Dr. Brennan, can America permanently defeat the Islamic state and other Islamic terrorist organizations without also defeating the underlying ideology that attracts so many fighters to their cause?

Mr. BRENNAN. The short answer to that is no. I mean, I think that what we find is that the—this is an ideology of revolution and during the late 20th century we had Marxism provided the ideology of revolution that went around the world. Today, this is it. We have to confront the ideology.

Mr. BROOKS. Dr. Rand, do you concur that the answer is no, that we have to defeat the ideology that breeds so many reinforcements to the Islamic state and other Islamic terrorist organizations?

Ms. RAND. Certainly, Congressman, and we are. This is one of the nine pillars and the areas where the coalition is working on the counter radicalization countering violent extremism and what is promising in this regard is some of the—our Arab partners are beginning and starting programs in their own countries to counter this ideology.

Recently, in Egypt, for example, a fatwa was issued against some of the ISIS ideology. It was unprecedented, in fact. Thank you.

Mr. BROOKS. With respect to Ambassador Jeffrey, Dr. Brennan and Dr. Rand, how can America best conduct itself to defeat the underlying Islamic ideology of the Islamic state and its brethren, Islamic terrorist organizations? Whoever wants to answer.

Ambassador JEFFREY. I will start. I agree with the problem. I would be very skeptical of the idea of we, the United States or the Western world, defeating a philosophical concept or distortion of a religion.

That is a very tricky thing. The vast majority of Muslims around the world are not our enemies. They look at their religion differently than the Salafists and the ISIS people and the people around the——

Mr. BROOKS. Okay. I am not asking for kind of an overall picture of what is going on. I am asking for what has to be done to defeat it.

Ambassador JEFFREY. Right.

Mr. BROOKS. I have limited time—40 seconds.

Ambassador JEFFREY. Fair enough. Stop the military manifestations of it, which is what we are doing with ISIS, which is what we are trying to do with Iran on nuclear weapons, and give the people of the region the space and support those who are strong in fending off this threat among themselves. That is all we can do.

Mr. BROOKS. Dr. Brennan, a few seconds left. How do we defeat the ideology?

Mr. BRENNAN. Continue to work with people like King Abdullah and President al-Sisi and develop that in other countries so that we have—the cure from this cancer comes from within Islam.

Mr. BROOKS. Dr. Rand, just a few seconds left. Any additional words?

Ms. RAND. I would add that the people in the Sunni heartland across Iraq and Syria they are mostly tribes. They don't necessarily inherently subscribe to this ideology.

So what we're trying to do is give them a chance. You know, they have been exploited too by the ISIS groups that are in their midst. So we are trying to help them.

Mr. BROOKS. Thank you, Madam Chairman, for the additional 15 seconds.

Ms. ROS-LEHTINEN. Thank you, Mr. Brooks.

Dr. Bera.

Mr. BERA. Thank you, Madam Chairman, and thank the witnesses.

Dr. Rand, was I correct in hearing you say we have been involved in 25 years of continuous engagement in Iraq?

Ms. RAND. To clarify, on and off for 25 years. I was counting the time at the beginning of the Gulf War, you know, which is—we are coming on to the 25th anniversary of the invasion.

Mr. BERA. Great. So on and off, and as we look at this current engagement it is accurate to say we are not talking about yours. We are talking about, you know, prolonged periods of times, perhaps decades. So no one disagrees with that.

Dr. Brennan, in answer to my colleague from Rhode Island, Mr. Cicilline, when asked about who can provide the numbers of ground troops in order to maintain stability, to create that open space, I think you characterized it as, you know, our allies in the region have limited capabilities, limited ground troops, and those ground troops largely are tied up within their own countries. Is that an accurate assessment?

Mr. BRENNAN. They are tied up but that doesn't mean that they can't provide some. What I think we have to have is reasonable expectations about what they can do based upon their own internal security interests.

Mr. BERA. So in this larger debate, you know, much of the debate is, you know, what the United States involvement is, what our troops' involvement is and no one is discounting that, you know, ISIL is—these are monsters.

These are despicable individuals. These are folks that are distorting a religion and we do have national security threats and we do have an interest in, you know, ridding the region of this ideology.

But it is not going to be easy and it is going to be prolonged and it is going to take decades. And, you know, I—you know, I disagree with my colleague, Mr. Salmon. I do think that it is our responsibility as Members of Congress to be engaged in defining the context of what this engagement looks like, not in prosecuting this—that is up to our military commanders, our diplomats and so forth—but engaging and I think the public wants us to be engaged in this definition. So I think that is a good thing.

This is not going to be easy and there, clearly, is a scenario. I think, Ambassador Jeffrey, you talked about, you know, some of the bad guys here—Assad, Iran, others.

But you can, clearly, see a scenario where you defeat ISIL, you drive them out, where you see this change from Iran to a Shi'a-dominated Iraq to Assad to Hezbollah to Hamas which, you know, we have to be conscious that that is one outcome here, which is not an outcome that I desire.

I think it is an outcome that, you know, puts some of our closest allies in a very precarious position and maybe even creates a worse scenario in this. So as we, Members of Congress, engage in this debate we have to be very conscious of all possible scenarios.

Ambassador Jeffrey, you touched on, you know, the lessons from Vietnam that, you know, I can imagine a ground campaign in Iraq with, you know, Shi'a militia, with Iraqi forces, with Kurdish fighters, a prolonged ground campaign that drives out Iraq. But the real challenge here is what happens in that bordering country, in Syria.

You know, there isn't a moderate Syrian force that can, you know, cut off that line of retreat. That then draws us into another rabbit hole and another prolonged scenario.

So, you know, I guess in the minute I have I think, starting with Dr. Rand, these scenarios that I am laying out are they inaccurate and the questions that we should be thinking about and asking?

Ms. RAND. Sure. Obviously, none of this is clear and that outcomes are not predetermined. You know, this is a very difficult region.

It is undergoing generational change in the form of the popular uprisings that have weakened state authority across the region.

We don't need to get into here all of the factors that are making this an unprecedented moment in the region and, of course, there is dangerous potential.

But, you know, the strategy is trying to figure out the political end game as I, you know, said in the written testimony in each of these particular feeders, and in Syria the idea of inserting a trained moderate opposition faction of 5,000 fighters is smart because this is the type of fighters that we could ally with.

These are the type of fighters that have a chance of reclaiming the territory once ISIS has been weakened in the areas.

Mr. BERA. But it will—it will take time. It will take time to train, to equip, to create this capable fighting force. Ambassador Jeffrey, and again, as I am thinking about this am I not laying—you know, am I thinking about this in the correct context?

Ms. ROS-LEHTINEN. Thank you, Dr. Bera, but your time is going to be limited.

Mr. Perry of Pennsylvania.

Mr. PERRY. Thank you, Madam Chair.

I would like to thank the panel for your service. Dr. Brennan, an additional thanks to you for your time in uniform.

I would like to associate myself with my colleagues Issa, Brooks and Higgins and their remarks, and just before I get started, regarding the contention that none of what we have tried in this arena has worked in the past and we tried to provide the breathing space, I think you must acknowledge that America was providing the support for the breathing space. Of course, it is not going to work when you walk away and no longer provide the support.

That having been said, to Dr. Brennan I think we have already agreed that, I think, ISIS—you know, we have agreed that ISIS is a symptom of a portion of—you know, a portion of a larger challenge.

Would you agree with that? I mean, I think you have said that before but I just want to clarify.

Mr. BRENNAN. I would.

Mr. PERRY. All right. And you said that it should be the first priority. I mean, you particularly said that.

Would it be fair for me to characterize—I think everybody is looking for a way to characterize it as a global violent jihad movement. Could that be a way of characterizing it?

Mr. BRENNAN. I think it is, but I think when you do that you also need to ensure that it addresses both sides of the equation.

Mr. PERRY. Sure. Sure. Absolutely. I mean, we also have kind of acknowledged that we are in the middle of a Shi'a-Sunni civil war, wahabiism, Sharia dogma. But let me ask you this. I mean, they fight each other.

They hate each other on occasion, what have you, but they see us, the West—the United States—as a common enemy where they will get together and fight us. Is that true or not true?

Mr. BRENNAN. I think if we are there in a large capacity that we will attract those forces who attack us. We had that situation in Iraq where we were both being attacked by the Shi'a extremists——

Mr. PERRY. But even if we are not there in large forces, I mean, they travel the globe looking for us and the West.

Mr. BRENNAN. We don't need to do anything for them to attack us.

Mr. PERRY. Right. We have already proven that, right? I mean, yeah. And people that say we have incited this and caused it I think that is a little specious.

Further, Dr. Brennan, the—you know we have already kind of broached the question the AUMF, why now, Article 2 powers, the first AUMF and, you know, I look at the administration's track record—look at it from a Member of Congress' standpoint.

Libya, Syria, Yemen, the side they chose in Egypt, what has happened in Iraq. We declare, he prosecutes. In my mind, he hasn't prosecuted very well. No disrespect intended but I just went down through the list.

Is there some rationale to thinking that the President might be looking for a complicitor in what has been in many people's minds a failed, an ineffective policy, strategy? I don't want to call it a strategy because I don't—a plan, an execution is something. I don't really see a strategy.

But we are going to get to that quickly. Is it—that a fair rationale? I mean, I am not saying it is not the end result but is it reasonable to think that people could feel that way?

Mr. BRENNAN. And not going to the motivation of the President——

Mr. PERRY. Sure.

Mr. BRENNAN [continuing]. I think it is fair to say that he is looking to have Congress as a participant in this process.

Mr. PERRY. Agreed. Can I stop you there, if I could? Ambassador, I agree with you that military force is not the only answer. You know, tediously, I am a student of Clausewitz. It is an extension of diplomacy.

That having been said, what about and where is the proper place for the associated actors here, here in this country and abroad, that enable, that fund, that support through fighters and material how should they be dealt with in an AUMF and if not where?

Ambassador JEFFREY. You mean the people who are supporting the ISIS movement?

Mr. PERRY. The people that support the global jihadist movement.

Ambassador JEFFREY. I think that the——

Mr. PERRY. And the organizations that have vowed publicly, that we let walk around among us, that we have in this building and down the street? What about them? Where do we deal with them if we are in this fight committed to winning and where is that in the strategy?

Ambassador JEFFREY. It is in the strategy, as my colleague pointed out. It is actually a nine-track strategy which internationally is a five-track strategy. But it is actually—it includes all of that.

The problem is some of this is political. Some of it is legal. For example, pursuing a lot of these people requires American laws and judicial action.

Mr. PERRY. With all due respect, so we have a couple hundred maybe or more unindicted co-conspirators in the Holy Land Foundation trial. They are walking around among us here and if you say this is a strategy that includes going after these people and deal—and that American laws are stopping us, there is one person that is stopping us.

It is the attorney general because he refuses to prosecute them. How do we feel—how do you explain to me that this is an authorization without a strategy—that strategy is an aspirational goal of defeating the enemy? That is it, because in reality we are not really going to do the hard things that need to be done.

Ambassador JEFFREY. I think the Congressional Record of Declarations of War and things like Declarations of War including this one have not tried to expand into these very complicated ideological, legal and other things but rather authorize the use of military force as part of that strategy. You need an explanation of that strategy.

You need an explanation of why those people have not been arrested and what we are doing about them as part of your analysis of our whole process here. But I wouldn't stick it in the legislation.

Mr. PERRY. Appreciate your thoughts.

Chairman ROYCE. Lois Frankel of Florida.

Ms. FRANKEL. Thank you, Mr. Chair, and thank you to the panel.

And let me just start. There are many folks on this panel who served our country. I want to thank them and those of you who have.

I come from a little different perspective because I have a son who I saw go to two wars. Sorry if I babble or get emotional. But I want to just say that I am lucky he came home safely.

I cannot tell you how horrific it was for his family. I don't even—so when I went to—and I think of the families who lost their children, their loved ones—the morbidity of the thousands of soldiers who returned and then we have to say what for.

So for me to make a decision of whether to send someone else's child into harm's way is, I think, the biggest decision or most important one that I will make in Congress. And I feel like we have been given this huge jigsaw puzzle where the pieces do not fit and my colleagues today have made a lot of—asked a lot of good questions, a lot of comments.

I can't repeat all of them but I have a number that I would ask you. You can just pick which ones you want to answer. I feel like we are in conflict all over the world and we have to have some strategy.

What is the most important enemy to be focused on? We are trying to prevent Iran from getting a nuclear weapon. Obviously, they are a player against ISIL.

We are trying to weaken Russia. Obviously, they are a player with Assad. That is just two examples. You have identified that we have to go after al-Qaeda as well. How does the—what we—the past AUMFs affect that and repealing that?

What about—is military action the only thing? I mean, how does humanitarian aid fit into this or educating women? I mean, is this the only way out and where does it leave us?

Who fills the void if we get ISIL? I mean, I could ask a lot more questions. So start with those and go at it.

Ambassador JEFFREY. While I criticized it earlier, the President's national security strategy does talk about that and it does a pretty good job and, you know, while I am a doom and gloom buy because that is where I have been deployed for many years, I will have to say this is a much safer better world now than it was when I started in this business as an army lieutenant in 1969 and that is largely because of the United States, the executive branch, the congressional support and the American people and what we have done.

So we—even though it is a jigsaw we don't like working in this jigsaw any more than you do observing it. We wish we could give you a clean sensible way forward and we are painfully aware we are not.

But that is how we have lived with and what we have seen in our lives—in my case, over almost 50 years now. We have seen a lot of progress and we have seen that smart use of military force with all of the other things you said combined, working with allies, actually does work.

We usually don't have the end game spelled out because we never know. We didn't have it spelled out with communism. We thought that we would contain it, push it back, go against it and hope for the best and it worked out.

That is about all I can tell you. But I am pretty optimistic in the long run. But I share your frustration at the jigsaw.

Ms. RAND. I agree about the complexity, Congresswoman, and I think you raise a lot of good—I like the image of a jigsaw puzzle. I think that is apt.

I would just offer that in this particular AUMF and that ISIS threat, in some ways there are three different theaters. I alluded to them before and it is helpful to me to think about them in terms of the partners and the objectives in Iraq, which differs significantly from Syria, which is much more complicated than Iraq in some ways—in many ways.

And then, finally, the third, which is the global contestation of ideas where there is a marketplace of ideas and change and social movements and Twitter and all kinds of youth bulges all over the world, not just the Arab world, that are leading to some of the radicalization causes so that the tools of U.S. statecraft need to be refined and specific to each of these three domains where our partners will be different, where our foes will be different, where the patrons of other foes will be different, et cetera.

Mr. BRENNAN. I would just add that it is a jigsaw puzzle. It is a very complex issue. But I think that that leads back to a piece I put in the paper, which is that we need to be thinking about how do you develop a grand strategy that moves us for the next 30 years as we address this issue.

I mean, we have the strategy of containment that came out of NSC–68 and the work of George Kennan and others.

We need to be doing that same type of thinking about this current world that we are in, how do we—how do we carry this forward using all elements, not just the military. The military is just one piece of the pie.

Chairman ROYCE. Okay. We go now to Mr. Reid Ribble of Wisconsin.

Mr. RIBBLE. Thank you, Mr. Chairman.

This has been really an insightful hearing and I thank all three of you for being here.

I would like to start with Dr. Brennan. We have heard from some of our colleagues here today that almost an implicit idea that we should just leave this to the region.

If we leave this fight to take care of ISIS to our regional partners and we just kind of step back out of it, one, what do you think would happen as a result of that strategy and would the U.S. homeland be put at risk implementing that strategy?

Mr. BRENNAN. Thanks for the question, Congressman. I think that since President Carter the United States has taken on the responsibility being the guarantor of regional security in that part of the world and we have vital interests both with our partners as well as in Europe and our own economy that are at stake here.

If we pull out it will create a huge power vacuum that will be filled by these very organizations that we wish to stop, so I think that would be the exact worst thing to do.

And the perception, unfortunately, from withdrawal of U.S. forces in 2011 by many of our partners in the region is that we are disengaging from the region.

We have to convince them that that is not true. Part of the way of doing that is by being more active in what we are doing in Iraq, showing that we are a commitment, the argument I made on putting troops on the ground, unless you put troops on the ground you aren't showing commitment or resolve and I think if nothing else that is one of the big benefits we will get out of this.

Mr. RIBBLE. Thank you.

Ambassador Jeffrey, in your written testimony in the second paragraph you talked about the campaign with our coalition partners and its strategy and I am going to quote out of here: ''Building up political capacity with our partners in Iraq and Syria'' is one thing you wrote, and then you wrote, ''Combatting the violent extremist ideology that fuels ISIS.''

Could you give us some specific ways that our partners along with the United States are combatting the violent extremist ideology and also could you tell us how successful our political capacity efforts in Syria are?

Ambassador JEFFREY. To start with the latter, they are not very successful. We don't have a good argument for the Sunni Arabs who are fighting against the Assad regime and simultaneously against the ISIS people, and our long-term program just to train a few thousand people is not an answer. What is our long-term vision of Syria?

We have a long-term vision for Iraq. I mean, I can spell it out. It is not too different than it has been since 2003 and it is sometimes ½, ⅓, 60 percent there.

That is a unified Iraq with the three groups living in something approaching harmony and the people we are supporting in Iraq including Prime Minister Abadi, the Kurds, many of these Sunni tribes, many of the other Sunni politicians I know, are working together to some degree better than in the recent past, certainly, and they are all opposed to this kind of violent extreme perversion of religion that we see in ISIS and that we see in Qom and Iran and they are our allies.

But they need a lot of support because if we did just walk away the bad guys win, as Dr. Brennan said.

Mr. RIBBLE. Is there a specific strategy, though, that you can use to combat the extremist ideology or is this just kind of flowery language that ended up in a strategy statement because it sounds good?

Ambassador JEFFREY. It is kind of like, only even more complicated, how did we—how did we respond to communism. There, that was different because it was an alternative vision of how we should live.

This is how these people should live and what they should draw from their religion. The basic—the first thing is fight those people who are coming out after us and coming out after the moderates.

Secondly, make it clear that this is not a war against Islam. We are not trying to take anybody's territory. We want to live in peace with the 1.4 billion Muslims around the world and support people who understand and get that—support them politically, support it through our propaganda, by our words, support it through our economic assistance and our diplomacy, and I think that this will work.

Mr. RIBBLE. Thank you.

Dr. Rand, a question specifically for you. You seem fairly supportive of the President's language in the AUMF. Why would it necessarily be bad for Congress to give broader authority than the President is even asking because he then would still have the ability to choose to restrain himself or not? Why is that a bad idea?

Ms. RAND. The AUMF is filling a lot of roles and we have talked about a lot of them today.

Mr. RIBBLE. Could you please move that closer to you so we can hear you?

Ms. RAND. The AUMF is serving a lot of roles and we have talked about a lot of them today, policy and legal. We haven't really hit on one of them, which is the legitimizing role it is playing and the message it is sending to our partners in this coalition and to the people in the region.

So there—enter the American public, which, by the way, public opinion shows—public opinion polls show are majority opposed to more extensive use of ground forces in this fight. So I think it hits the right target.

It balances between the need to send the message that we are not going to re-enter, re-engage the same kind of engagement boots on the ground that we have had for the past 10 years. It was deeply unpopular at home here in the United States and in the region.

Mr. RIBBLE. Mr. Chairman, I yield back.

Chairman ROYCE. Thank you. We go now to Mr. Gerry Connolly of Virginia.

Mr. CONNOLLY. Thank you. Thank you, Mr. Chairman, and welcome to the panel.

By the way, Ambassador Jeffrey, where are you from originally?

Ambassador JEFFREY. Just north of Boston.

Mr. CONNOLLY. Where?

Ambassador JEFFREY. Saugus.

Mr. CONNOLLY. Okay. I am from Boston.

Ambassador JEFFREY. Okay.

Mr. CONNOLLY. Thought I heard something similar. All right.

Dr. Brennan, I want to make sure I understood what you were saying about boots on the ground. Where and how many?

Mr. BRENNAN. What I have suggested that we would be able to do is——

Mr. CONNOLLY. And, again, if you could pull the microphone closer. Thank you.

Mr. BRENNAN. What I have suggested——

Mr. CONNOLLY. Perfect.

Mr. BRENNAN [continuing]. Is that the commanders on the field be allowed to have the types of capabilities that they need. I think——

Mr. CONNOLLY. Which—I am sorry—which field are we talking about?

Mr. BRENNAN. I am talking—we are talking about Iraq today.

Mr. CONNOLLY. Okay.

Mr. BRENNAN. And I believe what we need is to put—have a greater advise, train and assist role. We need to be able to put special operations forces down at the tactical level with our allied forces using A Teams and B Teams like they were meant to be used.

We may need to put supporting elements that are out there. In my view, we are probably looking at a package of somewhere between 5,000 and 8,000 troops. But, again, that is kind of a general range.

But the bigger issue is that is today, based on today's situations and conditions. As we get into the situation of having to take back Mosul, there might be a different need and different determination as necessary for that mission and I think the commanders need to be able to have the flexibility to come back and say this is what we need for success.

Mr. CONNOLLY. Okay. Gotcha. Thank you so much. And just a real quick question for you and then I want to go to Dr. Jeffrey, and do you agree that an AUMF is in order, holding in abeyance what should be in it and what shouldn't, but that the President is correct to seek one and we are correct to authorize one?

Mr. BRENNAN. I think it is very useful to go through this discussion and have this debate in terms of whether or not to deploy forces and if so how they should be utilized.

Mr. CONNOLLY. Thank you.

Ambassador Jeffrey, I heard you say, you know, we want to send the message to 1.4 billion Muslims around the world that we are on your side, this is, you know, not an adversarial relationship, there are some bad apples and let us all work together, Muslim and non-Muslim alike, to deal with the barbaric violence being perpetrated and the insanity being perpetrated by this group ISIS, and that certainly sounds good to an American audience.

But aren't we somewhat unwittingly the handmaidens of the creation of ISIS in that we so long supported the al-Maliki government that was perceived as absolutely hostile by the Sunni majority and in fact that hostility even today continues to fuel support even with the barbarity of ISIS and the violence of ISIS in the Sunni population because they are looking at what are my choices.

They are not looking at the nuance of the violence. They are looking at where do I throw my lot—where is my future and the choice is a hostile Shi'a government that absolutely is seeking to exclude me, if not worse, versus at least a Sunni group that is fighting on my behalf, allegedly, however violent it may be.

I am not justifying that but isn't that really what is going on in terms of what is fueling ISIS?

Ambassador JEFFREY. You are right, that is—that is how a lot of Sunnis think both about the Maliki government and about us. It is how the Muslim Brothers think about us in Egypt.

It is how, ironically, much of the Egyptian military who threw them out think about us. That is the problem and it is centered in your phrase supporting them.

We, and we means American Foreign Service Officers specifically as well as the administration and a lot of the pundits in the media, have given the impression that we actually make or break governments.

We really have very little control over them in the Middle East. The Iraqi people overwhelmingly voted for either a Shi'a party, a Shi'a coalition that Maliki was basically the head of, or a Kurdish coalition that for its own reasons in the end wanted to form a coalition with that Shi'a coalition.

That led to Maliki being in power. It was a democratic legally done thing. Although people argue about it, it is about as democratic and legal as anything gets in the Middle East.

The question is were we going to withdraw our support, overthrow it? How were we going to do that? I didn't have an answer and I was there. I tried as long as I could to find alternative candidates to—I was, to the extent I could, getting involved in the internal machinations of that society because we all saw problems with Maliki.

But we have Malikis all over the Middle East that we have to do business with because there are even worse people out there.

Mr. CONNOLLY. Well, and just to end on the note, you make a very good point. There is this assumption in large chunks of the world that we are somehow omnipotent and we most certainly are not.

Thank you.

Chairman ROYCE. We go to Mr. Lee Zeldin of New York.

Mr. ZELDIN. Thank you, Mr. Chairman.

I believe personally that it is good that the President has brought an authorization for the use of force against ISIS. My litmus test is going to be very simple—are we doing absolutely everything in our power to ensure that we win. I have some questions and concerns.

The President, in his original strategy back in September when he gave a speech, he was talking about dropping bombs and a reliance on Iraqi military and law enforcement to finish the job.

When I was in Iraq in 2006, it was an accomplishment to get them to show up to work. Expecting no threat that day, to get them to show up to a precinct that is a quarter mile from their house we were trying to get them to show up.

So relying on elements on the ground who have no morale, no patriotism, they don't have the resources, they don't have the training, they don't have the will is something that we have to take into account.

In that speech, the President said this was going to be different than past wars in Iraq and Afghanistan because there will be no boots on the ground, and in the same exact speech he says, tonight I am announcing 495 additional troops to Iraq.

Someone shows me a picture of their grandson in the Air Force. He is in Baghdad. He is wearing the uniform. He is carrying a rifle. He is wearing boots. Those boots are on the ground.

The use of this term ''boots on the ground'' here in Washington—the reality is is that we have boots on the ground right now and I think that we need to not worry about what polls say what wording sounds the best.

We also have to understand that we have some of the greatest special operation forces in the entire world. We have the best special operation forces in the entire world—Army Rangers, Green Berets, Navy SEALS, Marines, Delta Force.

When we talk about boots on the ground we are not talking about an enduring occupation. No one is talking about that. I don't support that.

But I will tell you what I do want—for a member of ISIS to sleep with one eye open because they fear an Army Ranger may be visiting their house or their fellow terrorist's house to put a round of lead between their eyes. We have to cut off logistics, command and control.

We have to find their funding streams and figure out how to cut them out. We need to increase our intelligence gathering abilities. These are all critically important. American exceptionalism isn't about strategic patience right now. American exceptionalism is about instilling fear in an element that does not respect weakness. They only respect strength.

Understanding that if we wait 5 years what we are going to be up against is going to be 100 times greater than what it is right now. I want to support the President's use of force.

I also want to do my due diligence. I want to know how many troops, which troops, what are their missions, who is in charge. Are they going to be given the flexibility and resources that are necessary to accomplish the task?

The President talks about necessary and appropriate in his resolution. What, to him, is necessary and appropriate? I'm going to read a letter that I just received, with my remaining time. I received this letter from someone who is watching. So there are people at home who watch these hearings.

He says,

> ''Lee, as a parent of a lieutenant in the Marines I have no doubt that if deployed he will do his duty with valor and distinction. However, unless, one, the President can specifically articulate our goals, two, the President explains the strategy specifically designed to achieve those goals and those goals include the utter destruction of ISIS wherever they function, and three, our troops are given whatever they need for however they long—however long they need it without limitation both as to weapons and tactics, I request that you vote against the authorization.

> ''The document as drafted appears to me to be an attempt to codify a failed strategy of limiting our ability to prevail. It is a political document which allows the President to say he cannot do more because Congress will not let him.

''He knows his strategy is failing and he needs someone else to blame. I will be damned if my son is going to be asked to risk his life for a failed strategy simply to allow the President to avoid the consequences of his incompetence. War is an all or nothing thing.

''Either authorize the full force, political, military and economic of the United States or do not send our troops in harm's way. We must fight to win or not fight at all.''

Our military has been outstretched. Lives have been lost. Limbs have been lost. Missed birthdays, missed anniversaries, missed holidays. We are not looking for conflict but conflict has found us and it is time for us to defeat ISIS.

We can't half ass it. We need to go all out and get the job done or not send our troops at all into harm's way. I yield back my time.

Chairman ROYCE. We go now to Ms. Grace Meng of New York.

Ms. MENG. Thank you, Mr. Chairman.

Thank you, Ranking Member Engel, and for all of our honorable witnesses for being here today.

I sort of want to piggy back off of what Mr. Ribble had previously asked about what coalition members should be prepared to do to continue delegitimizing ISIS' ideology. For example, a recent report indicated that around 4,000 foreign fighters have joined ISIS since the air strikes began.

Are there specific strategies that coalition members should be employing to further prevent the flow of foreign fighters into Syria and Iraq? And part two of that question is often talked about. ISIS calls themselves an Islamic state.

What name might you suggest we in America and around the world and in the media use to describe this barbaric group so as not to confer any undue sense of legitimacy? And anyone can——

Ms. RAND. Those are excellent questions, Congresswoman, and I would just add that I will defer the second one to my colleagues but the first one it is very interesting the types of political capital that is needed to be invested by leaders in the Arab Muslim world to fight—to counter radicalization, counter ideology.

Some of the examples I mentioned earlier were the leaders in Saudi Arabia and Egypt have helped their clerics issue fatwas condemning ISIS' violence, which is unprecedented.

There is also the importance of social media and the United States Government is not the only government that has the technical capacity to sort of tweet against ISIS. In fact, this is one sort of less reported part of the technical capacity building that is being done is we are helping our coalition governments build these anti-social media Web sites, et cetera.

It is a small thing but it is an important thing, given the percentage of the youth who are being radicalized in many of these societies. On the foreign fighters, my understanding is that the foreign fighters flowing into Syria and Iraq has been slowed in the past 3 or 4 months based on a couple of factors.

One is Turkey. We have increased our diplomacy or the coalition has increased its diplomacy in technical capacity building efforts with Turkey, and Turkey has improved its border security processes. So there is a lot of this that is technical that you need to do with partners.

It is better if it is done in a coalition so it is not just the United States telling people how to do better border security, how to fight foreign fighters.

And finally, I will just mention the U.N. Security Council resolution that the President introduced in September that was basically condemning and urging all member states to stop the flow of foreign fighters.

Mr. BRENNAN. Let me just go back to your question on the name.

I think we should join our friends—our Arab friends in the region and start calling them Daesh. They are not the Islamic state. They do not represent Islam.

They are an offshoot of that religion but they do not represent it and I think that we should—that would be a good way for us both in government and academia and others to try and show solidarity with our Arab allies.

But defeating the ideology goes back to talking—working with those leaders in those countries, helping them, supporting them, giving them the type of support that they need in the case of Iraq, and Iraq has a lot of problems and I am not certain where it is going to go.

Half the time I think it is going to survive and the other half I think it is going to fracture. But the reality is that we have invested $1 trillion and 1 million man years of labor and that there is a possibility that this may be saved, and I think if that is the case that we should continue to work on it and while—let me just go—take us just a little bit off for a second.

We missed a great opportunity in 2006 when the Maliki government needed us the most and didn't—and we did not push for reconciliation. I think at this point in time when the Iraqi Government needs us that a part of strategy has got to be and our support for them has got to be honest to goodness reconciliation that is not going to walk away from them as soon as the problem is over.

Ms. MENG. Thank you. And I will try to ask my last question fast.

Secretary Kerry previously testified that the U.S. would be resupplying the Iraqi Kurdish peshmerga going through Baghdad as so not to undermine the central government.

Has this arrangement prevented the Kurdish peshmerga from getting what they need to effectively fight ISIS and how would the central government in Baghdad view an effort to provide military equipment directly to the Kurds?

Ambassador JEFFREY. It did prevent the transfer of equipment when I was Ambassador. I don't have the statistics now but the Kurds certainly believe that it has.

They cite, as we heard earlier, only 25 of hundreds of MRAP armored vehicles that have been provided to them and while there are some pretty good reasons why we are careful in what we give them the point is they are fighting.

They are the allies of Baghdad and a lot of these weapon systems are no threat to Baghdad but they are a threat to ISIS and they should be flowing.

Chairman ROYCE. We will go now to Mr. Tom Emmer of Minnesota.

Mr. EMMER. Thank you, Mr. Chair, and I will try to be brief. I apologize for going back and forth. There seem to be a whole bunch of things going on at the same time, and I don't want to cover old ground but I am afraid I might touch a little bit.

My understanding, first, we are here because the President has requested renewed authorization for military force and it seems everything that I have read and everything that I have been listening to including your testimony everybody agrees that ISIL must be defeated.

There seems to be absolutely no disagreement. I heard today and I think this is for you, Dr. Brennan, if you would, and the others can certainly expand on it, you must first start by stopping the military manifestations and we have had reference to you have got to cut off the revenue sources, you have got to—I just wrote another one down listening to the testimony—we have got the ability to interrupt or interfere with Internet, social media, the like.

I would love to know to the extent this new authorization of military force, is that something that the administration is planning on doing on every level and how are we going to know what the strategy is?

Because I will tell you, I agree with my colleague, Mr. Zeldin from New York. I would offer that the executive should have all the authority that he needs to make sure that whatever the situation is, as fluid as it may be, you can deploy whatever resources are necessary to take the action that is necessary to win, not just hold something at bay, because—and I guess I will add this for the Ambassador.

I thought I heard you say earlier that we have never ventured into—that our country has never ventured into combating such a complex ideology, and all that came to mind was fascism and Marxism, and I would just ask you to help me with that because you have got that background. So, Dr. Brennan, could you fill us in? What needs to be done?

Mr. BRENNAN. I think the first thing that we need to do, and I think the President is doing this correct, is this is an Iraq first issue. How do you defeat ISIL—ISIS in Iraq? Do you go after their finances to the extent we can?

Much more complex than it was when we were there earlier because they now have $2 billion and they have their own revenue stream. But you use the Internet, the social media. You attack the ideology——

Mr. EMMER. Continue the air strikes?

Mr. BRENNAN. Enhance air strikes. I think we need to do much more in the way that we have been doing and but that will require, again, back to my point, you got to put boots on the ground, our forces with those forward leaning elements, not necessarily do the direct fighting but to be able to reach back and pull the resources of the U.S. Government.

I mean, one of the things on the AUMF that said the President was going to use our unique capabilities and I read that as being air enabled, and I got to tell you that U.S. ground forces capabilities, whether it be special forces, conventional forces or Army or Marine, are unique because it is not that one individual that you put out there.

It is that joint capacity that you bring to the battlefield, and that if we are going to make certain that our allies are going to be successful we got to be out there with them.

Mr. EMMER. So my question then, Dr. Brennan, because we are so limited on time, is if Congress is going to authorize the additional military force that the executive is asking for, why wouldn't Congress authorize the executive to take whatever action with whatever unique resources are available because this is such an immediate and dangerous threat not just to this country but the entire globe?

Why wouldn't the authorization be that broad?

Mr. BRENNAN. I, personally, think it probably should be that broad. Again, the President can restrict what he chooses to do but I think this AUMF is going to continue beyond this presidency and I think that what we shouldn't do is limit the next President based upon what this President may not want to do.

Mr. EMMER. Last question. And Mr. Ambassador, I am sorry if I am getting pinched. But that is what I would expect is the answer. Just common sense would tell me, not necessarily the experience, because I don't have yours.

But the only limitation—I am going to ask you if this is accurate or if you would disagree with this—the only limitation if there was one should be in the amount of time so that it has to come back to Congress for reauthorization and a discussion of what the strategy has been, where it has been. I mean, would that be the only——

Mr. BRENNAN. I think that would be perfectly acceptable to put a period of time.

Mr. EMMER. How long?

Mr. BRENNAN. I would go beyond the 3 years, maybe 4 years so the next President has some time to look at it, to revise the strategy and make the changes he needs before it comes to you.

Mr. EMMER. Thank you, and I—my time has expired.

Chairman ROYCE. Mr. Alan Grayson of Florida.

Mr. GRAYSON. Thank you.

Section 2(c) of the President's draft authorization for the use of military force reads as follows:

>   "The authority granted in subsection A does not authorize the use of U.S. armed forces in enduring offensive ground combat operations."

Ambassador Jeffrey, what does enduring mean?

Ambassador JEFFREY. My answer would be a somewhat sarcastic one—whatever the executive at the time defines enduring as, and I have a real problem with that.

Mr. GRAYSON. Dr. Brennan?

Mr. BRENNAN. I have real problems with that also, not only because it is—I don't know what it means. I could just see the lawyers fighting over the meaning of this.

But more importantly, if you are looking at committing forces for something that you say is either vital or an important interest of the United States and you get in the middle of a battle and all of a sudden are you on offense or are you on defense, what happens if neighbors cause problems? Wars never end the way that they were envisioned and so I think that would be a terrible mistake to put it in the AUMF.

Mr. GRAYSON. Dr. Rand?

Ms. RAND. Enduring, in my mind, specifies an open endedness. It specifies lack of clarity on the particular objective at hand.

Mr. GRAYSON. Dr. Rand, is 2 weeks enduring?

Ms. RAND. I will leave that to the lawyers to determine exactly.

Mr. GRAYSON. So your answer is you don't know, right? How about 2 months?

Ms. RAND. It would—again, I think it would depend on the particular objective. Enduring, in my mind, is not having a particular military objective in mind.

Mr. GRAYSON. So you don't really know what it means. Is that a fair statement?

Ms. RAND. Enduring, in my mind, means open ended.

Mr. GRAYSON. All right. Section 5 of the draft authorization of the use of military force reads as follows:

> "In this joint resolution the term associated persons or forces means individuals and organizations fighting for, on behalf of or alongside ISIL or any closely related successor ending hostilities against the United States or its coalition partners."

Ambassador Jeffrey, what does alongside ISIL mean?

Ambassador JEFFREY. I didn't draft this thing but——

Mr. GRAYSON. Nor did I.

Ambassador JEFFREY. Nor did you, but I would have put that in there if I had been drafting it and the reason is I think they went back to 2001.

Of course, this is the authorization we are still using along with the 2002 one for this campaign, and these things morph. For example, we have had a debate over whether ISIS is really a element of al-Qaeda.

It certainly was when I knew it as al-Qaeda in Iraq in 2010 to 2012, and these semantic arguments confuse us and confuse our people on the ground in trying to deal with these folks. You will know it when you see it if it is an ISIS or it is an ally of ISIS.

Mr. GRAYSON. How about the Free Syrian Army? Are they fighting alongside ISIL in Syria?

Ambassador JEFFREY. No, they are not fighting alongside ISIL. In fact, often they are fighting against ISIL and ISIL against them in particular.

Mr. GRAYSON. What about Assad? Is he fighting for or against? It is kind of hard to tell that scorecard, isn't it?

Ambassador JEFFREY. It sure is.

Mr. GRAYSON. Yes. What about you, Dr. Brennan? Can you tell me what alongside ISIL means?

Mr. BRENNAN. No, I really couldn't, and I think that what—you know, it might be—the 9–11 Commission uses the phrase radical Islamist organizations and I think maybe if we went to wording like that it includes all of those 52 groups that adhere to this type of ideology that threaten the United States.

But we are putting ourselves in boxes and, as you said, Congressman, I am trying to understand that means, what the limits are, who we are dealing with. It is very confusing.

Mr. GRAYSON. Dr. Rand?

Ms. RAND. Well, first of all, I believe that the confusion is probably a function of the fact that this is an unclassified document so it is not going to specify exactly which group or consider associates.

That would be for a classified setting. But, second, as I said in the testimony, the nature of the alliances within ISIL are changing and are fluid and those who are targeting—the military experts know exactly who is a derivative or an associate or an ally of ISIS at any given moment.

Mr. GRAYSON. Why are you so confident of that? It seems to me it is a matter of terminology, not a matter of ascertainable fact.

Ms. RAND. Based on my public service. I have seen some of the lawyers and some of the methodologies and——

Mr. GRAYSON. All right. Here is the $64-billion question for you, Ambassador Jeffrey, and then if we have time, for you others. If you can't tell us—you three experts can't tell us what these words mean, what does that tell us? Ambassador Jeffrey.

Ambassador JEFFREY. That it is very difficult to be using a tool basically designed to declare war or something like war on a nation state which has a fixed definition against a group that morphs, that changes its name, that has allies and other things.

Do we not fight it? We have to fight it. Are we having a hard time defining it? You bet.

Mr. GRAYSON. Dr. Brennan?

Mr. BRENNAN. I would agree with the Ambassador. I think the issue that we need to be looking at is trying to broaden terminology and understand that it is the tenets or organizations and groups that adhere to this ideology and make it broad enough that if one pops up in a different country that is doing the same thing that is a sister of this organization the President has the authority to act.

Mr. GRAYSON. Dr. Brennan, I think you just described a blank check, which I am not willing to give to the President or anybody else. But thank you for your time.

Chairman ROYCE. We go now to Mr. Ron DeSantis of Florida.

Mr. DESANTIS. Thank you, Mr. Chairman.

When the President addressed this issue in September, the White House said that he had authority to act based on the 2001 and 2002 AUMF, and so the media is reporting that he is asking Congress for authority.

But by their own view, he is asking Congress to restrict and limit the authority both by whatever—and I agree these are—these terms are nebulous but having some prohibition on the use of ground forces and having a time limit and I agree with the witnesses, I don't think that that is an effective way to fight an enemy.

I think you need to determine the enemy, determine the strategy and then bring all force to bear or be willing to do that and, obviously, the commander in chief needs to make these decisions.

But so I am trying to figure out what is motivating this and I think it is because if you look at the way things are going, if you look at the strategy that is in place or lack of strategy, this is not going to succeed and I think everybody understands that.

And so I think the President is looking to get Congress as imprimatur on his strategy so that he can then point the finger at us and say well, these guys limited me—I am just, you know, we all thought this was a good idea and right now he is kind of out there.

Congress is urging him to do different, and he gave an interview this week where he said look, you know, terrorism—the news makes a big deal about it—it is just something like a big city mayor—you know, you got to deal with criminals and such.

So I am thinking, like, Guiliani when he used to get these guys with the squeegees who would do that, I am, like, is that really how you are seeing it. So I am skeptical of the motivation for doing this now.

Let me ask you this, Dr. Brennan, because I think that this kind of informs where we are going. Is the problem a group of violent extremists who happen to be—go by the name of ISIS or whatever you want to call them, or is this a global jihad that presents national security implications and threatens our national security and our allies, not just in this part of Syria or that part of Iraq but really in countries across the globe?

Mr. BRENNAN. I think it is useful to look at this as not as a terrorist organization. It is a global phenomenon that we are seeing and I think you can also look at it as a global insurgency where you have sister organizations sprouting up all over the world fighting in support of the same type of ideology even though they may not have direct linkage or direct command and control.

Again, and I may use loosely the analogy of the 20th century when we had Marxist revolutions all over the world, many of them didn't like each other, didn't work with each other but they supported each other in different ways and I think that is the way of looking at it.

Mr. DeSANTIS. Dr. Rand mentioned, I think, accurately that a lot of these Sunni tribesman in Iraq, certainly, when I was serving there, they are really not jihadists. They are Sunni Arabs and if they think that back then AQI was better than the deal they get with the central government then they were out to do that and if they think it is a Shi'ite government then that is going to push them further.

So I guess my question is is if you look at the administration's policy there is a clear attempt to have a major rapprochement with Iran. If you look at Yemen now it could potentially be an Iranian client state.

The Assad—I know we have been through different machinations there but I think the administration is content to leave Assad there. And so if you are just the average Sunni Arab wanting to figure out should you kind of work with the Americans and whatever forces that we may be supporting or should you work with some of the Sunni jihadist groups, if they see us as a facilitating Shi'ite domination of the region isn't that going to push some of these Sunni Arabs who are not necessarily jihadists into the arms of the more radical Sunni groups? Ambassador?

Ambassador JEFFREY. Absolutely, which is why we can't pick a side in the Sunni-Shi'a struggle any more than we can pick a side in the Christian-Muslim struggle in the Balkans.

We have to have a set of values and friends who accept them and go after everybody who is violating them, whether they are coming out of Mosul or they are coming out of Tehran or they are coming out of Damascus.

Mr. DESANTIS. So if you have, for example, ISIS fighters threatening the outer Baghdad belts and you have Shi'ite militia groups, which we have considered to be terrorists when we were in Iraq and that are supported by Iran's Quds Force, some have said well, there is kind of an alliance with the U.S.—you know, we were supporting some of the anti-ISIS forces in other parts of Iraq and we were essentially relying on the Iranian-backed forces to keep ISIS out of Baghdad, is that a sustainable strategy?

Ambassador JEFFREY. In the long run, no. But there is a saying, you slay the wolf closest to the sled. Right now, when ISIS is moving forward we should be working with anybody that can stop them. But they have really not moved forward anymore. Now we got to figure out how to go get them and that is not——

Chairman ROYCE. Mr. Ted Deutch, the ranking member of the Middle East Subcommittee.

Mr. DEUTCH. Thank you, Mr. Chairman. Thanks to the witnesses for your willingness to come and stay through all these questions.

I would like to associate myself with many of my colleagues' comments on the tragic death of Kayla Mueller. I would also like to thank the chair and ranking member for working to ensure the committee has a strong voice in this AUMF process.

I welcome the President's request for an authorization for the use of military force against ISIL. We deserve to have a real and robust debate in Congress over the use of our military in order to ensure that our mission is clear and to ensure that past mistakes are not repeated.

I would like to follow up actually the last two members, both of my Florida colleagues had said, and I want to start by asking Ambassador Jeffrey in this discussion about whether ground troops are needed to combat ISIS.

We talk a lot about—the President has spoken a lot about letting our partners in the region take the lead. The question is what would be the impact of having Jordanian or Emirati troops on the ground.

What would the United States' role be in getting back to the back and forth that all of you had a little while ago? How would—would our role serving aside those troops in a—in something less than an enduring or could our role be described as anything less than an enduring end offensive role?

Ambassador JEFFREY. I think that—again, I didn't draft this thing but the drafters probably wanted to link enduring and offensive because we have an enduring presence in the Middle East. We have had combat troops in Kuwait for over a decade since I was there in the mid-90s. So it isn't a question of enduring.

It gets to could we use Jordanian troops. Absolutely, but there are lots of political problems and, frankly, we have never seen Arab troops on the offensive in any of our earlier wars, not in Iraq and not 2003 with a few exceptions, not in Afghanistan and not in Kuwait.

There are huge taboos about that in the Arab world. Some of them might be broken with some countries. My——

Mr. DEUTCH. Well, do you think—I am sorry. Do you think they have been? Do you think in light of recent events we wouldn't face those same political hurdles?

Ambassador JEFFREY. If I were advising the President I would say be very careful about that because the main value of these allies is their political support which plays well here and what they are doing in their own societies to deal with this violent Islamic manifestation.

If they start taking a lot of casualties in ground combat against ISIS, and they will—look at the Kurds, 500 or 600 killed—that is going to be very hard for them to sustain in their publics.

Again, as I mentioned in my opening remarks, these are countries that are very weak states. They have lots of problems internally.

Mr. DEUTCH. All right. So do you think, and I—Dr. Brennan and Dr. Rand—do you think, given the concerns Ambassador Jeffrey just laid out it is realistic to believe that a ground war could be fought by those troops without U.S. troops?

Mr. BRENNAN. I think U.S. troops have got to be there, and with the peshmerga we need to be—get out up front but even with the Iraqi military. As we start pushing into Anbar Province and especially as we start moving into some of the key cities and most importantly Mosul, it will be critically important to have our troops with them.

Exactly what that composition of troops is I think it depends on the situation at the time and the commander's analysis. But I think that if Congress is going to look at this and believe that this is something worth fighting for, then we need to give the commanders on the ground some flexibility.

Mr. DEUTCH. Doctor, and let me ask you something else, because I only have 1 minute left. This AUMF only deals with the 2002 AUMF. It doesn't touch the 2001 AUMF.

So the real question that I think a lot of us have is, as Congressman DeSantis said earlier, if the argument is that everything we are doing now we can pursue pursuant to the 2001 AUMF, then should we assume that whatever the limitations are that ultimately might be included in this AUMF, however broad those limitations are, that ultimately we could wind up doing anything we want pursuant to the existing 2001 AUMF anyway?

Ms. RAND. No, I don't believe that is the intention. I believe the intention is to make——

Mr. DEUTCH. No, no, no. I understand—I am not talking about the intention. I am asking whether you could still rely upon the 2001 AUMF to conduct whatever operations regardless of what is contained in here.

Ms. RAND. ISIS is a different threat than al-Qaeda. The 2001 AUMF——

Mr. DEUTCH. I—so you think no. Ambassador Jeffrey, you think yes?

Ambassador JEFFREY. Of course. The President has done everything he has done up to now, 2,000 air strikes drawing on that, and it is a very broad thing. I actually like it but I am having to give you an honest answer and, yeah, that is a problem.

Mr. DEUTCH. Thanks. Thank you, Mr. Chairman.

Chairman ROYCE. Okay. We go now to Mr. Ted Yoho of Florida.

Mr. YOHO. Thank you, Mr. Chairman. Gentlemen, ma'am, I appreciate you all being here.

Dr. Brennan, you said since the Carter presidency the U.S. have been the guarantors of peace in the region, and I look at Israel and Palestine, Syria with 220,000 dead plus, and we know the situation in Afghanistan, Iraq, Libya, Yemen, Lebanon. Jordan is a bright spot and let us not forget Iran. How do you assess we have done since the Carter administration?

Mr. BRENNAN. Well, I think our success rate has not been high.

Mr. YOHO. Okay. And I heard our President the other day say that if a failed policy like Cuba has not worked after 50 years it has to change.

I agree with that statement. I am not going to go into the Cuba debacle right now. Our whole process in the Middle East has to change because where do the ISIS come from? Dr. Brennan, you go ahead.

Mr. BRENNAN. Originally, it came from al-Qaeda in Iraq, then morphed into ISI, then later into ISIS.

Mr. YOHO. And then if we go back to what the President is saying here, that we are going to degrade and defeat ISIS, I remember those statements in the Iraq War, Mission Accomplished. But we weren't done.

I remember this President saying al-Qaeda is on the run, they are the JV team, they are gone. And the question I have for all three of you is what is the definitive definition of defeat of ISIL. Because ISIL is an ideology.

We are not fighting a nation state. It is like fighting a tumor that metastasizes and we are going after the metastasis—we are not going at the root cause.

So I would like to hear a definition of defeat, a definitive one, and then I would like to hear what your root cause is of why there is an ISIS, why there was an al-Qaeda, and I have got one other question after that. Ambassador, if you would go first.

Ambassador JEFFREY. It is a good point and it is the major flaw of this draft. The draft doesn't tell. You give this back to the President and it doesn't authorize the President to do anything more than using armed forces against ISIL.

It doesn't say defeat, although that is one of the things that he says is his goal or working to defeat in the Whereas. So there is no goal. One of the reasons we have all been debating about how long this thing should be or whether—what kind of troops and what enduring the hell means is that there is no goal.

My goal is to defeat ISIS, is to destroy its hold on Tehran and Iraq and Syria. That is what should be in this thing. That is a military mission. We can do it, if possible, with our allies.

Potentially, we will have to use our own forces. If that is a vital mission that is what the President should be tasked to do by you.

Mr. YOHO. I think you are absolutely right, and if we don't define what ISIL is as a radical Islamic jihadist group you can't—you can't defeat it.

It is like let us build a house and I give you a bunch of two by fours and the material and you are, like, well, what is the plan—I don't know, just build a house, and that is what I see here. I know that is a simple analogy or a bad analogy but I see us wanting to commit but not really wanting to commit.

It is like you are not playing to win—you are playing not to lose. And it is just if we are not going to go in there with a very specific strategy this is a bad idea. Dr. Brennan, what is your opinion?

Mr. BRENNAN. I agree with that and I think that what you need to do to defeat Iraq and Syria or ISIS is to understand that we are putting, at some level an artificial distinction, at the border between Iraq and Syria.

We have to look at the entire organization. I agree Iraq first, but we need to be thinking about how do we attack this entire organization and make certain that it no longer controls territory. And the Ambassador is exactly right, that is a military objective.

But it means that we have to be able to move into Syria also.

Mr. YOHO. Which is attacking a sovereign state. It may be a failed state but we are attacking that and that just opens up a whole another can of worms.

Mr. BRENNAN. Absolutely.

Mr. YOHO. Dr. Rand, go ahead and weigh in on that.

Ms. RAND. I would just disagree with my colleagues in the sense that I——

Mr. YOHO. Did you say disagree?

Ms. RAND. I would disagree in the sense that I think the strategy—there is, again, preliminary evidence that it is working. This is what the military advisors to the President are recommending as a way to defeat the enemy, right.

So this combination of limited U.S. force with air strikes paired with the coalition partners on the ground has killed 7,000 ISIS fighters out of an organization that——

Mr. YOHO. How many have grown out of that, though? Every time you kill one you get 10 or 20 more that join the cause. So are we winning?

Ms. RAND. And has helped the Iraqi forces—the partners—the Kurds and the Iraqi security forces retake key strategic areas. So in my mind, the strategy should be assessed based on how well it is working and so far in 5 months I think there is limited and preliminary but significant evidence that this combination of limited U.S. force and partners is working.

Mr. YOHO. I appreciate your time. I am out of time. Thank you, Mr. Chairman.

Chairman ROYCE. I thank the member from Florida.

Well, we appreciate the time of all of our witnesses here today and this was a start of a very important conversation.

So I think as we deal with this—deal with this growing threat from ISIS and as we deal with the President's request we thank you again.

We are going to be submitting some additional questions to our panel. I appreciate your response, and we stand adjourned.

[Whereupon, at 1:01 p.m., the committee was adjourned.]

APPENDIX

————

MATERIAL SUBMITTED FOR THE RECORD

FULL COMMITTEE HEARING NOTICE
COMMITTEE ON FOREIGN AFFAIRS
U.S. HOUSE OF REPRESENTATIVES
WASHINGTON, DC 20515-6128

Edward R. Royce (R-CA), Chairman

February 12, 2015

TO: MEMBERS OF THE COMMITTEE ON FOREIGN AFFAIRS

You are respectfully requested to attend an OPEN hearing of the Committee on Foreign Affairs, to be held in Room 2172 of the Rayburn House Office Building (and available live on the Committee website at http://www.ForeignAffairs.house.gov):

DATE: Thursday, February 12, 2015

TIME: 10:00 a.m.

SUBJECT: The Growing Strategic Threat of ISIS

WITNESSES: The Honorable James F. Jeffrey
                   Philip Solondz Distinguished Visiting Fellow
                   The Washington Institute for Near East Policy

                   Dafna H. Rand, Ph.D.
                   Leon E. Panetta Fellow and Deputy Director of Studies
                   Center for a New American Security

                   Rick Brennan, Jr., Ph.D.
                   Senior Political Scientist
                   RAND Corporation

By Direction of the Chairman

The Committee on Foreign Affairs seeks to make its facilities accessible to persons with disabilities. If you are in need of special accommodations, please call 202/225-5021 at least four business days in advance of the event, whenever practicable. Questions with regard to special accommodations in general (including availability of Committee materials in alternative formats and assistive listening devices) may be directed to the Committee.

COMMITTEE ON FOREIGN AFFAIRS
MINUTES OF FULL COMMITTEE HEARING

Day___*Wednesday*___Date____*April 12, 2015*____Room_____*2172*_____

Starting Time___*10:04 a.m.*___Ending Time___*1:01 p.m.*___

Recesses___*0*___(____to____)(____to____)(____to____)(____to____)(____to____)(____to____)

Presiding Member(s)

Edward R. Royce, Chairman

Check all of the following that apply:

Open Session [✓]   Electronically Recorded (taped) [✓]
Executive (closed) Session [ ]   Stenographic Record [✓]
Televised [✓]

TITLE OF HEARING:

The Growing Strategic Threat of ISIS

COMMITTEE MEMBERS PRESENT:

See Attached Sheet.

NON-COMMITTEE MEMBERS PRESENT:

None.

HEARING WITNESSES: Same as meeting notice attached? Yes [✓] No [ ]
(If "no", please list below and include title, agency, department, or organization.)

STATEMENTS FOR THE RECORD: *(List any statements submitted for the record.)*

None.

TIME SCHEDULED TO RECONVENE_____
or
TIME ADJOURNED *1:01 p.m.*

Jean Marter, Director of Committee Operations

HOUSE COMMITTEE ON FOREIGN AFFAIRS
FULL COMMITTEE HEARING

PRESENT	MEMBER	PRESENT	MEMBER
X	Edward R. Royce, CA	X	Eliot L. Engel, NY
X	Christopher H. Smith, NJ	X	Brad Sherman, CA
X	Ileana Ros-Lehtinen, FL	X	Gregory W. Meeks, NY
X	Dana Rohrabacher, CA	X	Albio Sires, NJ
X	Steve Chabot, OH	X	Gerald E. Connolly, VA
	Joe Wilson, SC	X	Theodore E. Deutch, FL
	Michael T. McCaul, TX	X	Brian Higgins, NY
X	Ted Poe, TX	X	Karen Bass, CA
X	Matt Salmon, AZ	X	William Keating, MA
X	Darrell Issa, CA	X	David Cicilline, RI
X	Tom Marino, PA	X	Alan Grayson, FL
X	Jeff Duncan, SC	X	Ami Bera, CA
X	Mo Brooks, AL	X	Alan S. Lowenthal, CA
X	Paul Cook, CA	X	Grace Meng, NY
X	Randy Weber, TX	X	Lois Frankel, FL
X	Scott Perry, PA	X	Tulsi Gabbard, HI
X	Ron DeSantis, FL	X	Joaquin Castro, TX
X	Mark Meadows, NC	X	Robin Kelly, IL
X	Ted Yoho, FL	X	Brendan Boyle, PA
X	Curt Clawson, FL		
X	Scott, DesJarlais, TN		
X	Reid Ribble, WI		
	Dave Trott, MI		
X	Lee Zeldin, NY		
X	Tom Emmer, MN